The New Testament Experience of Faith

by Leander E. Keck

THE BETHANY PRESS
St. Louis, Missouri

Library of Congress Cataloging in Publication Data

Keck, Leander E.
   The New Testament Experience of Faith

   1. Bible. N.T.—Criticism, interpretation, etc.
   2. Christianity—Origin. I. Title.
BS2361.2.K42   225.6   76-46491
ISBN: O-8272-2507-5

Cover design by Terri Kurtz

Contents

For my three brothers

Byford Osburn
Donald J. Keck
John A. Osburn

One by blood, two by law

Chapter One

CHRISTIANS BEFORE THE NEW TESTAMENT

It's easy to take the New Testament for granted. After all, it's been around for a long time. Is it possible to read it as if it were just off the press? Perhaps. Much depends on how we come at it.

To read the New Testament with a sense of discovery may require a new relationship to it. On the one hand, for many people the New Testament is basically a stranger, like one of our neighbors. We know he is there, have some impression of him, and a few occasional encounters with him, but we really do not know him. But after extended conversation one can say, "Now I think I begin to understand him." For such readers, this book may serve as a kind of "open house" where the strangers can get to know one another better. The "one another" is important, because in getting to know the New Testament we also get to know something about ourselves.

On the other hand, those who have been reading the New Testament for a long time may have a sense of discovery by approaching it from a different angle, by stepping back so to speak, in order to see it in a different light. By getting "distance" on the familiar we come to know it better. For instance, the students who leaves home for college soon understands the family in a way not possible otherwise. Whoever we are, a sense of discovery may require a new relationship to the New Testament.

Discovery includes an element of surprise. One may discover that "distance" and "nearness" (long-standing familiarity) are reversed. Those who thought they were strangers may find that they have far more in common than they expected. Those who thought they already knew the New Testament may be surprised by what is in it.

5

Actually, we can speak of a double surprise. First, the closer we get to the New Testament the farther away from us it appears to be. Once we begin reading it carefully and asking certain questions about it, we discover that it is at home in a different world. It takes for granted beliefs that some of us no longer hold (demons, for example). It talks about things we are not interested in (whether one may eat meat which has been "sacrificed to idols"). It ignores problems for which we seek guidance (abortion laws). It assumes what we have rejected as evil (slavery), and urges what many find offensive (subordination of women). How can such a book be of any help today? Why should people want to know "what the New Testament says about . . ."? The discovery of this kind of distance between ourselves and the New Testament is too common an experience to be swept under the rug. Indeed, it is to be encouraged if we really want to understand it.

Second, by discovering the distance between ourselves and the New Testament we also find ourselves in it. As we shall see, the New Testament is a series of "answers" to particular questions. This suggests that we grasp the "answer" only if we first see what the question was. By stepping back from the answers to see the questions we discover that many of them are like our own. By getting acquainted with the early Christians we discover that people "back there" faced some of the same problems we do. They too had to deal with conflicts in the family over political ideas, hostility from neighbors who did not understand what following Jesus may require, conflict over the proper attitude toward sexuality or the place of women in the church. After discovering what was going on in the early Christian communities we may feel more at home there than we expected to, even though their world remains distant from ours.

It is the questions of the early Christians that link us to the New Testament. Because the New Testament deals with the issues before the early Christians, the more we discover similarities between their issues and ours, the more we discover that it addresses us too. This book aims to make such discoveries easier.

To start this process, the present chapter will first clarify the relation between the New Testament and the early Christians in order to show how we can use the New Testament to study them. After explaining why this approach does not call into question the inspiration of the Bible, we will get an overview of early Christianity by noting four factors which affected their development. Then we shall focus attention on the development of early Christian beliefs. Finally, we shall make some suggestions about the use of this book for the reader's own study.

THE NEW TESTAMENT AND THE EARLY CHRISTIANS

The first step in getting some distance on the New Testament is to see how it was related to the early Christians. The New Testament is so much a part of Christianity today that it is hard to imagine Christians and churches existing without it. Yet for the first hundred years or so, Christianity flourished without the New Testament. To be sure, by the end of this period (around A.D. 150) every book in our New Testament had been written, and many of them had been used in churches for decades. But they were not used because they were part of the New Testament; rather, they became part of the New Testament because they had been used regularly.

Making the Christian Bible

Actually, we cannot speak of the New Testament until we reach that point where these Christian writings were placed alongside the Old Testament in order to make a Bible in two parts. Until then, the churches used a one-part Bible, the Scriptures of the synagogues, what we now call the Old Testament. Indeed, exactly which writings made up this Bible was not yet decided because Jews of the Aramaic-speaking synagogues of Palestine used a shorter collection than did the Greek-speaking Jews. The former used a Bible which is identical with that of the Protestant Old Testament (but in different order), whereas the latter used the Greek translation which is more or less identical with the Catholic Old Testament (the Apocrypha is included).

The point is that the Bible of the early Christians was the Bible of the synagogue. Some Christian writings came to be used alongside it, and later the church determined that the Christian Scripture would include both. Not until then can we really speak of the Old Testament and the New Testament.

Christianity did not arise when people began believing the New Testament. Mormonism can be regarded as a faith which is a response to a book, but not Christianity. Christianity emerged when people believed a message, the gospel. What that gospel was we shall discuss later. Just now we need to see that the New Testament did not generate the church; rather, it was the church that generated and defined the New Testament.

How the church came to have a two-part Bible is a fascinating story, and only two highlights can be mentioned here. First, declaring the synagogue Bible to be the Old Testament was the outcome of a long struggle which split many churches. The synagogue Bible had been taken for granted as the Scripture of the church for a century. Then there appeared a Christian teacher named Marcion (around A.D. 140), who insisted that this was all wrong.

Marcion was convinced that Jesus came to save us from this evil world which the Creator, the God of the Jews and of the Old Testament, had made. Faithfulness to the gospel, as he saw it, required the church to repudiate the world and its Creator, as well as the Old Testament, because the true God sent his Son to liberate us from this bondage.

Christians must have their own Scripture, which Marcion provided: the Gospel of Luke and the Letters of Paul. Since these letters quoted the Old Testament favorably, Marcion concluded that they had been tampered with. So he edited out these passages (and deleted parts of Luke as well), in order to create a purely Christian Scripture. Many churches followed, but eventually Marcionism was overcome. In the process, the church insisted that the synagogue Scripture would be called "The Books of the Old Covenant" (Testament).

Second, in rejecting the Scripture of the Marcionites the church gradually determined which writings would constitute the "Books of the New Covenant," and their order as well. It decided that the New Testament would have four gospels instead of one, and the letters of apostles besides Paul (and it rejected the "purged" form of Paul's letters put out by Marcion). However, it followed Marcion in having a "gospel" part followed by an "epistle" part of the New Testament. It also used the Book of Acts as a bridge between them, and eventually it ended the collection with the Book of Revelation.

The most important decisions had been made before the end of the second century, but in the case of some books, such as James or Revelation, it would be several hundred years before all the churches accepted them. In fact, the oldest list of New Testament books which is identical with the Table of Contents we know comes from A.D. 367, but even this list was not accepted everywhere at the time.

No one set out to write the New Testament. What we have is a collection made under particular circumstances. If we were to discover for the first time a copy of the New Testament in a bookstore, we might expect it to be a rather different book. Some things which we might expect to find in it are not there. There is no collection of hymns or prayers, no manual of organization for the church, no summary of beliefs required by all, no order of

8

worship. Instead, there are only three kinds of literature: narratives, letters, and a report of a series of visions.

Of the five narrative books, one deals with early Christians while the other four tell about Jesus. Most of the letters claim to be by one man, Paul. Yet he was not among Jesus' original followers. The New Testament is a book weighted in favor of Paul; thirteen letters are attributed to him but only two to Peter, and over half of Acts is devoted to Paul as well. Did Paul overshadow Peter in the early church as much as he does in the New Testament? With this question we are on the border of the next set of considerations.

Using the New Testament to Study the Early Christians

Since the New Testament books were responses to the problems of the early Christians, telling the story of the early Christians properly requires us to get their situations and difficulties in proper order. Otherwise we would attribute to one generation the problems of another. The resulting confusion would be like trying to use Martin Luther King's "Letter from a Birmingham Jail" in order to understand the background of Lincoln's "Emancipation Proclamation." In other words, since the problems of the early Christians are known chiefly from the New Testament, we must put these writings in the correct sequence. Then we can write the history of the early Christians.

The books of the New Testament do not stand in the order in which they were written. If we were to put them into such an order, the list would begin with First Thessalonians and end with Second Peter. Putting the New Testament books in their historical sequence would show us important things about the New Testament. It would also have important consequences for the way we go about studying the early Christians. We shall look briefly at both results.

What would such a list show us about the New Testament? Even though Jesus lived and died before Paul, all the Gospels were written after Paul's death. Thus the oldest books of the New Testament are from Paul. Since the Gospels were written after Paul (from about A.D. 70-100), where did they get their information about Jesus? They either copied older accounts or put into writing what had been handed down by word of mouth. Actually, the Gospels contain both oral tradition and earlier written materials, as we shall see.

From the first generation we have only the letters of Paul. Most of the New Testament comes from the second generation (about A.D. 70-100), and a good deal from the third (roughly A.D. 100-

140). None of the books of the New Testament come from the earliest church in Jerusalem. Although the Epistle of James implies that it was written by James, Jesus' brother who became head of the Jerusalem church, the Epistle does not say so itself. Today scarcely any scholar thinks that Jesus' brother wrote it. The same is true of Jude. Both come from a much later time. In antiquity, writing books in the name of famous people was not regarded as an act of dishonesty but as a way of honoring them by allowing them to speak to a later generation.

What are some of the consequences for studying the early Christians? First, we have much more material from the later decades of the New Testament period than from the early ones. Thus far we have spoken only of the New Testament books, but actually they represent only part of what early Christians wrote by A.D. 150. By then there were other gospels, other letters, and other books of revelation and "Acts." Some of this literature is just as old as the later books of the New Testament. For example, the First Letter of Clement was written about the same time as the Revelation to John (about A.D. 95–96). Consequently, to understand the Christians of this period, we cannot restrict ourselves to the New Testament alone.

Second, if we take account of all Christian literature up to A.D. 150, and if we succeed in putting it more or less in right historical order, then we can see some patterns. On the one hand, we can see which problems disappear and which ones keep coming back. One which disappeared was whether gentiles can be Christians without becoming Jews as well; that was settled fairly early, though not without a struggle—as we shall see in chapter three. One problem which keeps coming back has to do with the proper Christian attitude toward the Roman empire. On the other hand, we see more than one pattern because Christianity was diverse, not uniform. We do not see a single development, but different trends going on at the same time. Thereby the rich diversity of early Christianity comes into focus.

Third, the extent of our information varies from place to place as well as from time to time. Therefore, we must also try to put the literature in its proper region or city. This is often difficult to do. Roman historians barely mention Christianity for it was not yet important enough in their eyes to write about.

Fourth, in studying the early Christians and their literature we work with degrees of probability. Our most solid ground is with the letters of Paul because we know when they were written and to whom they were sent. But much early Christian literature is anonymous, and we are not sure where it was written or, in the

10

case of letters, to whom they were sent. None of the Gospels names the Evangelist who wrote them; the names by which we know them were added later, perhaps correctly in some cases. But a good guess, even an ancient one, is not the same as good evidence.

This book cannot discuss these problems fully, or even mention all of them. It will, however, indicate the writer's judgment on such matters so that the reader can see the basis for what is being said. For example, it is *possible* that the Gospel of John was written at Antioch; it is *probable* that Matthew also was produced there, and there is *no doubt* that Paul wrote I Corinthians at Ephesus.

Uncertainty at some points will not prevent us from venturing inferences about the early Christians. After all, that is how one tries out possibilities, tests hypotheses. Besides, it is by asking new questions that the New Testament will open up to us in a fresh way. In the long run that is what matters most.

Are We Forgetting Something?

We have already covered a lot of ground. What could we have overlooked? Some persons might be asking whether, in stepping back in order to see the New Testament in relation to early Christianity, we have not overlooked the claim that God had a hand in it all. Or to put it more conventionally, have we forgotten the Holy Spirit?

This is an important question, especially in light of the long-standing conviction that the Bible is inspired. Often it is called "the Word of God." The question is significant because it points to a whole bundle of issues, none of which can be discussed adequately here. Still, the central issue needs to be focused more sharply and several observations made.

In approaching the New Testament by way of the early Christians and their circumstances are we leaving out the element of inspiration? Does studying the New Testament as one would read Shakespeare in light of contemporary English life actually take away the inspiration of the Bible? Because many people have thought so, we cannot bypass the question. Such persons feel that if one can understand the New Testament without appealing to its inspiration, then somehow inspiration has become unnecessary.

However, several observations may put this feeling into a different light. First, it is poor strategy to use inspiration to explain things in the Bible or about the Bible. On the one hand, this will inevitably put inspiration at the mercy of explanation. The more one can explain historically, the less will be left for inspiration to account for.

11

This way of approaching the matter inevitably dooms inspiration to some sort of theological game preserve where it is protected artificially from extinction. Experience has confirmed this in many ways. For example, it used to be thought that the peculiarities of New Testament Greek, when compared with classical Greek, resulted from inspiration. But then it turned out that the Greek of the New Testament was the ordinary spoken Greek of the time, and had nothing to do with inspiration. Inspiration is not what we use to fill the gaps of our information.

On the other hand, using inspiration to explain things is bad theology because it mixes two categories of thought. Indeed, it makes God a factor in the chain of cause and effect, whereas God is actually to be confessed as the ground of all causes and effects.

Moreover, explanations have to do with causes and effects, with questions like Who?, What?, or Why? These are historical questions and must get an historical answer, insofar as possible. For instance, the question, Who wrote Ephesians? is a strictly historical one and must be answered on the basis of evidence and argument which a historian will honor. The inspiration of the Bible cannot guarantee that the opening line of this book, "Paul, an apostle of Christ Jesus" is historically correct. Inspiration does not explain or guarantee anything historically. It is a way of making a confession of faith, namely, that through this book we encounter God.

In the second place, therefore, explaining how the New Testament came to be the sort of Scripture it is has nothing to do one way or other with the inspiration of the Bible. In developing our approach, we have not neglected something; we have deliberately excluded it because it is not relevant to the task at hand. In the last analysis, the only person who can really say that the New Testament is inspired is the one who has been inspired by it— and that is a statement of faith. Explaining things about the New Testament can neither make this experience happen, nor prevent it from occurring. In fact, many have found that they are inspired more as their understanding grows. Inspiration and ignorance are not identical twins; they are not even related, though they sometimes have the same address.

Finally, while explanation does not prevent inspiration, it does affect the concept or idea of what inspiration involves. The foregoing paragraphs are Exhibit A of this. The remarks that follow may be considered Exhibit B, namely, liberation from the idea that the inspiration of the Bible guarantees the historical accuracy of every word.

People who insist that every word is factually accurate because all the original words of the Bible are inspired forget the key thing —we do not have the original words. What we do have is thousands of manuscripts which disagree among themselves considerably over what it was that Paul, for instance, wrote. Every New Testament which one can read, including one in Greek, prints somebody's judgment about the wording because no perfect manuscript exists. There is no other New Testament. (Many newer translations print the different wording in the footnotes.) There is no point in claiming that the original text was error-free if no one has seen it for eighteen centuries.

Once one sees that inspiration did not provide us with error-free manuscripts, then we begin to understand the concept of inspiration differently. It is no longer linked with accuracy, freedom from error, and the like. Now "inspiration" is free to mean something more profound religiously—that the reader believes God speaks to him or her through the text because God had spoken to the writer. Theologically speaking, the Word of God is free. When that Word happens to us, we know what the inspiration of the Bible really means.

FROM SECT TO NEW RELIGION

It is important to have an overview of the major developments in the rise of Christianity before we turn to particular circumstances. In this way we can see where the individual parts fit and also note certain elements to which we can refer later.

The Standpoint

In speaking of early Christianity in terms of a development from sect to religion, several things are implied. One, Christianity did not begin as a new religion but as a Jewish sect. A "sect" is a group, usually small, which claims that its understanding of the religious tradition is the only true one. A religion, on the other hand, is a system of beliefs, practices, rituals, and organizational structure (if it has one). A sect usually exists within a religion because a sect does not challenge the whole system, but it insists that certain emphases represent the true form of the religion which is otherwise shared.

Sects magnify their distinctive emphases because without them they would lose their reason to exist. They do not want to include differences, but to exclude them. Consequently, sects tend to recruit their members from those who otherwise share the general religious tradition. Because sects regard themselves as representing the true (and usually original) form of this religion, they do not call themselves sects. For example, one could call Primitive Baptists a sect because they view other Baptists as having strayed from the true, Calvinistic theology, and as having wrongly abandoned foot-washing. At the same time, they are not a religion alongside Christianity because they share the same Bible, the same general view of Christ, and some common practices.

Two, although Christianity began as a special group within Judaism, it became a religion which was conscious of being independent of it, with its own Scripture, belief-system, rituals, and organizational structure. The transformation of the sect into a religion was a long and complex process, and doubtless proceeded differently from place to place.

Three, to speak of the change from sect to religion is not to pass judgment on this shift, to say that it was "good" or "bad." It is common, of course, to regard the earliest form of Christianity as the purest and to view with regret most subsequent developments. Protestants regularly have wanted to "get back to New Testament Christianity" because they believe that the New Testament is the norm by which the church judges itself.

This view is based on the assumption that early Christianity and New Testament Christianity are the same thing. But there are problems with this. First, the New Testament understanding of Christianity is not one thing but several things, and it changed from one generation to the next. To which "New Testament Christianity" does one wish to return—that of the Jerusalem church, that of Paul's churches, or that of Rome in A.D. 95? If one assumes that the earliest is the purest, then it will turn out that this is the most impossible of all to recover, for this was a sect at home in a Judaism which is gone forever.

Second, it is not really possible to equate "New Testament Christianity" with "early Christianity." Actually, one must distinguish one from the other because the New Testament books were written largely as critiques of early Christianity. The New Testament does not simply express what early Christians were, but also criticizes them for what they were. Besides, the norm of the church today is not the early Christians but the New Testament. Once we find out how similar are the problems of the first-century Christians to our own, it becomes clear that we are already more like the early Christians than we ought to be.

Third, the repeated call to return to the original form of Christianity implies that there was a golden age of the church, a time when faith was pure, convictions strong, and prayers effective. It also implies that ever since some sort of "fall" of the church we

14

have had to make do with a pale copy of the original. But, as we shall see, the early Christians were far from perfect. They were as prone to bickering, faithlessness, misunderstanding, and struggles for power as later generations. Besides, one cannot regard the early church as the golden age of Christianity without slipping (unnoticed) into the implication that the Holy Spirit faded out, or that in later times the Spirit becomes effective only now and then, whereas "back there in New Testament times" it was effective constantly.

Just because we stop viewing the early Christians as the ideal Christians, the "real" Christians in contrast with 99% of those who came later, we need not accept every later development uncritically. Some developments had long-lasting, favorable results; others did not. Is this not true of any period in history?

Factors in the Development of Early Christianity

We shall call attention to four factors: the role of Judaism, the religiosity of the gentiles, the institutionalizing of Christianity, and the change in Christian expectation of the Lord's coming. First, the role of Judaism in Palestine differed from that of the Greek-speaking Jews of the diaspora (=dispersion). Since we shall look more closely at the Palestinian scene in the next chapter, we can concentrate here on the diaspora.

For centuries thousands of Jews had lived outside Palestine. We were concerned here with that wing of the diaspora in the cities of the Greco-Roman world. The main Jewish communities were found in Alexandria in Egypt, in Antioch in Syria, and at Rome. Each had its own character, the Alexandrian being the largest and most influential.

To varying degrees, they were Hellenized—that is, influenced by Greek life, language, and thought. By New Testament times, Jews were found in virtually every ctiy of the empire, and some had been Hellenized for generations. The Jews of the dispersion varied among themselves as much as do present-day Jews in New York. Some carefully preserved traditional Jewish ways, while others abandoned their Jewishness altogether and were assimilated as thoroughly modern, first century, secularized persons. In between were various efforts to define what it meant to be a Jew in the Greco-Roman world.

Many diaspora Jews had double names, one Jewish, and a Greek or Latin name as well. One of these was Saul of Tarsus, ᾽whose other name was Paulus. Like many others, he was bilingual, able to use both Greek and Aramaic, and perhaps a bit of Hebrew as well.

15

Diaspora Jews who were faithful to the Jewish religion organized synagogues, which were centers of Jewish religious life and learning. Ever since the third century B.C., they had been using the Greek version of the Bible, the Septuagint, which had been translated in Egypt. Loyal Jews collected money annually which they sent to the temple in Jerusalem—a sign of their solidarity with their brothers in the homeland. Those who could afford it went to Jerusalem for the Holy Days such as Passover or Pentecost; others actually moved there, as did those mentioned in Acts 2:5.

The diaspora Jews evidently were missionary-minded, for we hear frequently of gentile converts, proselytes. Other gentiles were attracted to Judaism, attended synagogue worship and observed some of the customs, but refused to be circumcised. These were welcomed by the synagogue and were known as "God-fearers." (Notice how according to Acts 13:16 Paul addresses both Jews and God-fearers.)

In the spread of Christianity, these Hellenistic synagogues played a key role. They were the natural points of contact for Christian missionaries who were Jews themselves, and the God-fearers probably formed the core of many new congregations. In seeking converts, these synagogues developed typical ways of presenting Judaism favorably to their gentile friends. Christians often adopted the same approach and even teaching materials, and simply Christianized them as needed. Moreover, the God-fearers already regarded the Jewish Bible as Scripture; therefore Christian preachers did not need to introduce it first before preaching from it. They simply had to interpret it in a new way.

In short, the Hellenistic synagogues prepared the way for Christianity, though of course they did not intend to do so. It is hard to imagine how Christianity could have spread so rapidly had the Hellenistic synagogues not been there.

A second factor has to do with the religiosity of the ordinary gentile in the same Greco-Roman cities. It is difficult to generalize accurately about popular religion of the day, but some features do stand out.

Christianity entered a world that was, like our own, simultaneously very secular and very religious—depending on whom one is talking with. Skepticism was widespread, for many of the old religions had lost their power over the lives of people. On the other hand, this same experience made others seek a religion which satisfied their needs. Some were turning to astrology as never before. Others were eagerly seeking out the cults in which they underwent elaborate rituals. These are the famous "mystery religions." Not much is known about them because participants were sworn to secrecy—and they kept their vows. In any case, every city offered as many religious options as does the church page in a metropolitan newspaper today.

People assumed that miracles were part of religion. Stories of miracles were standard fare in attracting adherents. Reports of healings, visions, resuscitations from the dead were regarded as "evidences" of the truth and power of a given religion. Not surprisingly, there were also charlatans. We hear, for instance, of a ventriloquist who invented a "talking snake" in order to get his own religion going. We should not be surprised to find miracles popular in early Christianity. Compared with some later Christian literature, the so-called "apocryphal New Testament," there are relatively few miracle stories in the New Testament. There is nothing comparable to the story of the apostle who, finding bugs in his bed, ordered them all outside for the night, where they stood in rows until morning!

It was taken for granted that certain religious rituals had power, including power to make one immortal. In some of the mystery religions, it was believed that when one ate the flesh of a slain animal one was eating the god himself. Only to a few philosophers did it occur to point out that rituals are symbols of spiritual truths. The ordinary person regarded the ritual as doing something, not as standing for something. In other words, religion was profoundly sacramental. In Chapter 4 we shall see what sorts of problems this will create for the way baptism and the Lord's Supper were understood in Corinth.

Even though we have scarcely scratched the surface, enough may have been suggested to show that Christianity entered a world that was receptive to a message of personal salvation. At the same time, this very receptivity had its dangers. One of the most persistent dangers was a turn of mind, an outlook, which regarded the material world, including one's physical body, as evil and believed that one's soul was an eternal, divine spark which was a stranger in the world. To such a mentality, nothing was more important than the salvation of the soul from the body. Known as Gnosticism (from *gnosis,* the Greek word for knowledge), this mentality grew ever stronger in the same period that Christianity developed, and so had a profound effect on the way Christians responded to the gospel.

Whereas the first two factors we have mentioned can be regarded as external to the church, in the sense that they were part of the scene before Christianity emerged, two others are internal

17

ones. The third has to do with the tension between ardor and order, between the inspiration of the Spirit and the needs of the institution. In other words, a third formative factor is the gradual institutionalization of Christianity.

New movements often appear to be chaotic to outsiders, and are sometimes experienced this way by insiders too. But gradually what was once exciting and new becomes routine. Out of many gifted persons a leadership emerges, which in turn is more careful about procedures and lines of authority. The Christian movement was no exception to this prevailing pattern, and one cannot expect that it should have been.

Right from the start, it was a common Christian conviction that everyone who was baptized received the Holy Spirit, the power of the coming New Age. Some persons apparently were specially endowed and were known as prophets; many spoke in tongues, at least in Paul's churches. So long as the congregations were small, relatively new and enthusiastic, and so long as they had an apostle or his associate to guide them, everyone could participate in the affairs of the group. They were united in the Spirit.

But things could not stay this way. The apostle or his associate may leave. Who is in charge then? Even activities believed to be inspired by the Spirit become habitual and routine. Then new persons join the group who, in the name of their own inspiration, want to make changes. As tensions arise, people discover that appealing to what the Spirit told them solves nothing, because both sides claim to be inspired. So other bases for settling such questions must be found.

Normally, these new bases concern respect for the leadership which was properly chosen, and for following approved procedures. So it was in the emerging church. In short, early Christians found that being saved and receiving the Spirit did not transplant them into churches that were free of problems; they were not *that* saved! So gradually concern for order replaced reliance on ardor.

In the New Testament we see numerous signs of this process. In Paul's time, there seem to have been no "offices" in the church, no grades of clergy; instead, everyone used the Spirit-given gift for the common good (1 Cor. 12). Later, when the Letter to the Ephesians was written (probably by a follower of Paul), the gifts of the Spirit are said to be distinct offices: apostles, prophets, evangelists, pastors, teachers (Eph. 4:11). Later still, when 1 Timothy was penned, we not only hear of bishops and deacons as distinct offices, but get a list of qualifications, and not a word is said about having the Spirit!

Doubtless the writer of 1 Timothy would not have denied that bishops and deacons have been given the Spirit. He clearly reflects the wisdom of experience which has shown that having the Spirit is not enough to determine who is qualified and competent (1 Tim. 3). In fact, it is precisely people who claim the Spirit who are causing problems for the writer of 1 John: "Beloved, do not believe every spirit, but test the spirits to see whether they are of God; for many false prophets have gone out into the world" (1 John 4:1).

Later we hear that there were charlatans among the prophets too. Since there was a long-standing tradition of being hospitable to wandering men of God, some apparently knew "a good thing" when they saw it. Therefore a teacher whose writing is not in the New Testament advised that if a prophet stays for more than three days or asks for money, send him packing!

In view of what was said above, it is clear that one should not simply bemoan the institutionalization of Christianity as "the fall of the church." This was inevitable and necessary, given the problems created by the view that everyone receives the Spirit. Instead of idealizing the situation in Paul's time, one might well ask the opposite question: How long could one lead a church where everyone did his own thing in the name of the Spirit?

Indeed, in view of the actual problems which the church faced, one should also ask whether, and to what extent, the church was being faithful to the gospel in a new sense by moving toward order and structured accountability. Or, on the other hand, is it the case that institutions inevitably frustrate what they set out to preserve? It is worthwhile to see how the early Christians struggled with these questions, for they are also ours.

A fourth factor was the change in early Christian expectation. Since we shall encounter aspects of this repeatedly, it is enough simply to call attention to it here. At the outset, Christians believed that the Lord would return soon because this conviction was bound up with believing that Jesus had been resurrected (see p. 22). Twenty years later, Paul still believed that he would live to experience it (1 Thess. 5:1-18). However, the Lord did not come when expected.

Inevitably, Christians made various adjustments to this fact. One of these was increased concern for the structure and order of the church as an institution which would continue indefinitely, as we have just seen. Another was a growing sense that the End was postponed but that in the meanwhile the gospel must be preached to all nations (Mark 13:10). As a result, the Coming became one

19

of the things Christians still believed in, but was no longer the center which affected everything else.

A third adjustment had to do with the relation to the world around them. Whereas Paul could urge that Christians not take social involvements too seriously because this world is passing away anyway (1 Cor. 7:25-31), two hundred years later Christians were claiming that they were holding society together. Eventually, they would try to build a Christian civilization. The beginnings of this development can be found already in the latest parts of the New Testament.

Development of Christian Beliefs

Christianity did not begin with the full body of beliefs we know today. Rather, in the course of many years, the characteristic Christian doctrines developed from their beginnings in the New Testament period.

The "apostolic benediction" in 2 Corinthians 13:14 is a clear example: "The grace of our Lord Jesus Christ and the love of God and the fellowship of the Holy Spirit be with you all." Paul apparently never felt the need to spell out exactly how God, Christ, and the Holy Spirit are related to one another, but when later Christians began to hold different views on the subject, a debate emerged which resulted in the doctrine of the Trinity. "Trinity" is not a New Testament word, yet this doctrine attempts to say how various statements in the New Testament are to be understood.

The important thing to see here, however, is that Christian beliefs began to develop right from the start. The New Testament therefore embodies various stages of development. It is difficult to speak of *the* New Testament belief or theology because there were different theologies being developed in the early church. Naturally, they overlapped a great deal. But still, one should not assume that the theology of Paul was identical with that of John or Matthew.

It is useful to note several factors that affected the development of Christian beliefs generally. In this way we will learn what to look for in the process.

Since Christianity began within Judaism basic Jewish beliefs were taken for granted, such as the authority of the Scriptures, the special place of Israel, and the existence of but one God. Marcion was such a threat because he denied all these beliefs. To understand the development of Christian doctrines, we need to keep our eye on the way this Jewish legacy was appropriated.

Taking the gospel to gentiles of the Greco-Roman world required the apostles to put the message in ways that non-Jews could

20

grasp. Thus the Hellenization of the gospel began. Even the same words did not mean the same thing in Jerusalem and Corinth. A well known example is "son of God." In Jewish thought, any person who was especially obedient to God and lived a godly life could be called "son of God"; Jesus used the phrase this way in Matthew 5:44-45. But in the Greek world, a person who was God's son was somehow divine. Thus we should be alert to the ways evangelizing gentiles affected Christian beliefs.

We should also take account of the controversies among early Christians. One does not need to spell out exactly what a belief means until it is challenged. Thus, early Christians did not doubt that the same God created the world and sent his Son. But when Marcion insisted that Jesus was not the Son of the Creator but of another god, it was necessary to clarify the issues and say what must be said. For example, the Apostles' Creed insists that God is "maker of heaven and earth" and that Jesus Christ is "his only Son." These words are repeated casually today; in the second century they were "fighting words." The more we learn about Christianity, the more alert we become to the ways Christian beliefs were clarified by controversies.

In short, the beliefs of the early Christians are not to be taken for granted. They certainly did not do so. Christian theology emerged in controversy from the start. The reason is as clear as it is important permanently: Christianity did not begin as a new form of worship nor as a proposal to find something more meaningful. It began as a controversial conviction. From the start, it was what one *believed* that made a person a Christian. A religion which begins this way will inevitably make beliefs central—if it breeds true to itself.

The rest of this book will show us the circumstances in which various Christian beliefs were being developed. Here we can limit ourselves to outlining the starting-point, the central beliefs of the earliest community in Jerusalem. The earliest Christian theology was thoroughly Jewish. What distinguished some Jews from all the rest was what they believed about Jesus. To an outsider, say a Roman historian, that would have been a minor difference. But to those involved, everything turned on this axis—though it would be some time before all the consequences became clear.

Unfortunately for us, the earliest Christians did not write down exactly what they believed. The Book of Acts tells us some things, but it was written 50-60 years later, probably by a gentile living outside Palestine. But we are fortunate in having an outline of their distinctive beliefs because Paul quotes it, and adds his own comments in 1 Corinthians 15:3-11.

21

This is a carefully worded piece of tradition which Paul acquired when he became a Christian—doubtless within five years of the beginning of the church. This means that we are in direct touch with what the earliest church regarded as crucial. It is helpful to print part of it here so that its structure stands out.

> . . . Christ died for our sins
>   in accordance with the scriptures
> he was buried
> he was raised on the third day
>   in accordance with the scriptures
> he appeared to Cephas
>   then to the twelve. . . .

This passage contains the essentials but not all of them, because there is no mention of the coming of the Holy Spirit, nor of baptism. The fact that it ignores the life and teachings of Jesus may surprise us at first, but not when we reflect on it. This is a summary outline of what had to be asserted in a situation when all of these points were controversial (except Jesus' burial). Jews who were not believers denied them all. On the other hand, no one doubted that Jesus had lived in a certain way or had taught certain things. But in that situation what made one a member of the Christian community was believing these statements and what they meant.

The pivot on which these beliefs turn is Jesus' resurrection. Time and again, we shall see, the resurrection had to be interpreted afresh as new questions arose. Just now, however, we want to know what it meant for first century Jews to believe that Jesus had been raised from the dead.

• Most Jews believed in resurrection before they heard about Jesus. Apart from wholly secularized Jews of the day, it was chiefly the Sadducees who denied there was such a thing as resurrection. (See Mark 12:18; Acts 23:6-8. The Sadducees were the wealthy priests: for a fuller discussion of groups within Judaism, see chap. 2.) Resurrection was one of the things expected to occur at the End, along with the Last Judgment and the arrival of the New Age.

Today, many persons have trouble believing there is such a thing as resurrection. For most Jews in A.D. 30 the question was not, Is there a resurrection?, but rather, Has resurrection happened? Some were saying that it had, and that it had happened to Jesus.

- By saying "was raised" instead of "he arose," Christian Jews were saying that it was God who resurrected Jesus. Jews often used the passive form of the verb in order to avoid mentioning God explicitly (see also Mark 4:11). To say that God raised Jesus, however, was to say that God had not repudiated him, even though he had been crucified as a criminal.

If God resurrected Jesus, then the End-time must be beginning. The curtain must be going up on the New Age. An illustration may help. If a visitor to Washington, D.C. sees a platform being erected on the east steps of the capitol, he assumes that there will be an inauguration, and that there will also be a parade, speeches, and an inaugural ball, because all these things go together. Likewise, for a first-century Jew to believe that there had been a resurrection (and not a mere resuscitation) was to believe that the New Age is under way at last.

- If the New Age is dawning because of Jesus' resurrection, then he must be the Messiah. One can also turn it around and say that then the Messiah must be Jesus! Also according to Acts 2:36 it was the resurrection that installed Jesus into the office of Messiah. The earliest Christians did not believe Jesus was the Messiah (or, Christ) because they remembered his ideas on the subject, but because they believed God had raised him from the dead and conferred this office upon him. At his coming, his Messiahship will be manifest.

- If all this be true, then Jesus' death must have been more than a miscarriage of justice. It must have been necessary in God's mysterious ways, for without it the New Age would not have come by his resurrection from the dead. Since the New Age is necessary because human sin corrupted the present Age, Jesus' death was for the sake of our sins. The earliest Christians did not yet have a "doctrine of the atonement," but what they believed about Jesus' death led to one.

- All this must agree with the Scriptures. Those who rejected the claims about Jesus' resurrection naturally denied that the Bible pointed to these things. Thus the phrase "in accordance with the Scriptures" reveals a battleground with non-believers. It also began a long process of Christian reinterpretation of the Bible; calling it the "*Old* Testament" is a stage in this process.

Whenever these beliefs have been retained, Christianity has kept its links with Jewish theology, which was their original matrix. At the same time, every element in this old tradition was the basis of further development of Christian theology, some of which is apparent already in the New Testament.

A GUIDE TO THE GUIDEBOOK

We have seen some aspects of approaching the New Testament by way of the early Christians for whom it was written in the first place. What now remains to be done in this chapter is to indicate what we shall and shall not undertake in this book.

First, one cannot study early Christians in general any more than one can study twentieth-century Americans in general. In both cases there are too many differences from place to place and from generation to generation. So we shall organize the material on the basis of particular places. We shall look at Christians in Palestine, Antioch, Corinth, western Asia Minor, and Rome. Furthermore, we will try to distinguish one generation from the next, even though sharp lines cannot be drawn between them.

In the second place, we shall not discuss every book or every issue Christians faced. That would double the size of the book. Nor would it be necessary for a new understanding of the New Testament. We shall therefore select some representative material. Even so, some topics appear in more than one chapter because Christians in more than one place had to deal with them. Cross-references will aid the reader to review the theme and make some comparisons.

Third, this book is really a guidebook to the New Testament itself. This manifests itself in several ways:

Only rarely is the New Testament quoted fully. By no means must this be taken to mean that one can dispense with it in order to stick to this book. To the contrary! The New Testament text needs to be read—preferably in more than one translation.

Where a passage is analyzed in greater detail, the discussion can be followed only if the New Testament itself is at hand. In this way the reader begins to participate in the study.

Finally, only occasionally will this book point out the relevance of the material for today. To do so repeatedly would be preaching—in the best sense, by the way! Nevertheless the book does not intend to address the readers, but to aid them in discovering for themselves both the difficulties and the possibilities of appropriating the New Testament today. When that happens, the purpose of gaining distance will be achieved.

But there must be an easier way! There is. The writer of this book could tell the readers what it all means and how one goes about "applying" it. But that would take all the fun out of it—for both of us.

Chapter Two

CRISES OF THE WAY

Every one of the earliest Christians were Jews. In fact, they did not even know they were "Christians" because this name was created later in Antioch, evidently by outsiders (Acts 11:26). In Jerusalem they came to be known as "the sect of the Nazarenes" (Acts 24:5). Apparently they did not give themselves a single name, but regarded themselves as the Messiah's people (saints), and as followers of "the Way" (Acts 9:1-2).

What distinguished them from their fellow Jews was what they believed about Jesus (see p. 21). Gradually the onsequences of these beliefs became apparent, as they faced the question: How does believing in Jesus affect Jewish customs and religion? To understand the earliest believers we must look at certain aspects of Judaism of the time.

JEWISH SOIL OF EARLY CHRISTIANITY

The early church emerged within a Judaism that was both frustrated and fragmented. This frustration resulted from political circumstances. Ever since Alexander the Great conquered Palestine in 332 B.C., the people were exposed to Greek ways. The Greeks Hellenized the world they mastered just as we have Americanized the non-Communist world. Many Jews in Palestine adopted Greek ways, while others did not. After Alexander's death, the vast empire was divided among his generals; the family of Ptolemy ruled Egypt, and the family of Seleucus ruled Syria and eventually conquered Palestine. In order to consolidate his rule over Palestine, Antiochus IV forbade the practice of Judaism altogether in

168 B.C., and had a pig sacrificed in the temple. The result was insurrection, known as the Maccabean war. In three years the Jews rededicated the temple, still celebrated by the festival of Hanukkah in December. The Books of 1 and 2 Maccabees in the Apocrypha tell more about this period, as does the Book of Daniel, which writes about it in symbols.

Finally, independence was won in 142 B.C. However, the new Jewish kings were sometimes as tyrannical as the Greeks had been, and some Jews became quite disillusioned with what the war of liberation had produced. In 63 B.C. the Romans arrived, and from then until A.D. 1948 there was no independent Jewish state in Palestine. The Romans ruled first through local puppet kings, the most famous being Herod, in whose reign Jesus was born. Later, Rome ruled directly through Procurators, the best known being Pilate, who executed Jesus.

Increasingly Rome's heavy-handedness caused unrest. At last, in A.D. 66 the First Revolt broke out. When it ended four years later, Jerusalem had been captured, the temple burned and looted, its contents shipped to Rome. In A.D. 132-35 the Second Revolt broke out. This time the results were worse: the city was destroyed, a pagan temple replaced the old one, the new city was renamed Aelia Capitolina, and Jews were forbidden to live there on penalty of death.

In short, from 168 B.C. to A.D. 135 Palestine endured unrest and repeated war. Christianity was born in tumultuous times which provided one crisis after another for the Way.

In this setting, Judaism became fragmented, as one group after another put forward its understanding of how to cope with the situation. By the time of early Christianity, we can distinguish six types of responses, though there was a good deal of overlapping.

• Some Jews virtually gave up their religious traditions and became "modern *secular* persons," virtually indistinguishable from the many gentiles who now lived in Palestine, especially in Galilee. Some became secularized because they had adopted Greek ways, others because they were simply too busy making a living to care about religion. These were called "the people of the land," and Pharisees regarded them as rednecks.

• The *Hellenized Jews* tried to practice Judaism while at the same time living more or less as Greeks. There were numerous synagogues in Palestine where Greek was used and the Bible read in Greek.

• The *Sadducees* were also Hellenized, but they represented the wealthy priestly and aristocratic families. Being responsible for public order, they cooperated with the Romans so that the temple

26

sacrifices would not be interrupted. Besides the temple also served as the bank (see 2 Mac. 4), and financial institutions tend to adjust to political realities in order to assure stability. Religiously, the Sadducees were traditionalists. They regarded only the Pentateuch (the first five Books of the Bible) as Scripture, and they denied the resurrection because it was not taught in these Books. These "law and order" Jews had no sympathy with Messianic hopes.

• Although the temple was the central institution, the actual religious life of many people was shaped by the synagogues of the towns. It was here that the *Pharisees* exerted their influence. The Pharisees were fraternities of teachers and students devoted to the study of Torah and to working out the details of what full obedience required. They believed that the Torah had two forms—what was written in Scripture (the same Books as in the Protestant Old Testament), and what had been handed down by word of mouth. Their aim was to make the whole nation obedient to Torah; this meant extending to everyone the laws which originally applied only to the priests. In this way, all Israel would be a holy people. They were prepared to tolerate the Romans so long as the people were free to practice Judaism.

• Others were persuaded that one could not be a faithful Jew and remain in society. So the *Essenes* withdrew to Qumran, near the Dead Sea, to set up a commune. This group may have originated in the disappointment over the outcome of the Maccabean war. In any case, they believed that the temple was in the hands of the wrong priests, that the religious calendar used in Jerusalem was wrong, and that they alone were the true Israel. Their literature, the "Dead Sea Scrolls," was discovered in 1947.

• Finally, the militant nationalists would not tolerate Rome, and despised those who did. As Roman policy became more oppressive, they formed the *Zealot* underground in the years leading up to the First Revolt. Not all Zealots were religiously motivated, but many regarded rebellion as a holy war.

After the First Revolt, the community at Qumran was gone, the Sadducees disappeared, the Zealots were killed; but the Pharisees survived and put their stamp on subsequent Judaism. It was from them that rabbinic Judaism emerged.

Aspects of Judaism

It is difficult to get an accurate picture of Judaism before the First Revolt (A.D. 66-70). The Dead Sea Scrolls are so important because they give us direct information about a Jewish sect of the

27

time. Very important are the writings of Josephus, a general in the First Revolt who defected to the Romans and then lived on a government pension in Rome and wrote the history of the war and of the Jewish people. His account is rather biased, for he does not blame Rome but Jewish radicals.

Unfortunately, we have no comparable account about the Second Revolt (A.D. 132-135). We do have a vast amount of rabbinic material, much of which tells about the early years of the first century. But all of it was compiled after the Second Revolt and so reflects the way the later rabbis wanted the tradition to be understood.

In short, apart from the Dead Sea Scrolls we have only very limited direct access to Judaism as it existed in the time of earliest Christianity. Later materials must be used with great care because Judaism changed fundamentally after the Fall of Jerusalem.

For our purpose, however, certain basic things are clear enough.

• Judaism emphasized the religious importance of the nation, the people and its land. The various groups were at odds with one another because each had a different view of what being the people of God required. Those at Qumran regarded the rest as apostates, the Zealots disagreed with the Pharisees and Sadducees over the attitude toward Rome, and the Sadducees resented the Pharisees. Yet all emphasized the nation.

• Jewish religion was more concerned with doing than thinking, more with orthopraxy (right practice) than with orthodoxy (right belief). There were only two unquestionable beliefs: God is one, and Israel is his chosen people. So long as these were not threatened, Judaism could tolerate a wide range of ideas and practices because doing the right things in the right way at the right time was important for everyone. What one believed about the Sabbath was not as important as whether one observed it properly. What divided people was what "properly" meant.

Judaism was not concerned only with externals. To the contrary, a great emphasis was placed on attitudes and motives, especially by Essenes and Pharisees. Both were deeply concerned for the life of prayer and devotion. For them, obedience to the law was a privilege and a joy, not a burden. The common people, however, may well have found the Pharisees' interpretations burdensome.

• The religious festivals were central and were celebrated in the temple at Jerusalem. Passover in the spring and the Day of Atonement in the fall were the chief ones, as they still are. The Sabbath (from sundown on Friday to sundown on Saturday) provided weekly worship and instruction at the synagogues. After the

28

temple was destroyed, the festivals were celebrated in homes and synagogues.

• Many Jews hoped for deliverance, and for a God-sent Messiah to lead them to freedom. But not all shared this hope (the Sadducees saw it as subversive), and the people at Qumran expected two Messiahs, a priestly as well as a political one. There were many forms of messianic hope, but in no case did Jews expect a Messiah who was a divine savior from individual sins. After the Second Revolt, the rabbis repudiated Messianism in order to build a nation of law-observing people under Roman, and later under Christian, rule.

How did Judaism react to the new sect which claimed that the Messiah is Jesus, soon to return in power? Understandably, there were diverse responses. On the one hand, the believers in Jesus were tolerated in the synagogues for a long time because they continued to be practicing Jews. Not until about A.D. 85, when the rabbis were consolidating the Jewish community after the war, were Christians squeezed out. A basic prayer of the liturgy was expanded to include a curse on the heretics; since the Christians knew it was aimed largely at them, they could no longer participate.

On the other hand, there were degrees of harrassment from the start. Families were divided and friendships broken. Paul the apostle first appears as a Pharisee persecuting the church (Acts 8:1-3; 9:1-2). Curiously, neither he nor Acts explains why he did so. Perhaps he regarded as blasphemy the claim that a man crucified was the Messiah, and he saw the emerging Christian life-pattern as a threat to the Torah. This chapter aims to discern something of that developing pattern of life and the crises in which it was wrought.

THE TRUE ISRAEL

The expected time of redemption is here! That was the central meaning of God's raising Jesus from the dead and installing him into the office of Messiah (see p. 23). Soon he would come in power to complete his work. With this message Jesus' followers sought to persuade their fellow Jews to prepare for the New Age by becoming part of the Messiah's people.

The Way of the Messiah's People

This was a remarkable message, for it did not fall within the range of Jewish expectations of the Messiah, diverse as they were. Actually, because Jesus had been executed one might argue that he could not be the Messiah because the Messiah was to liberate his people from Rome and rule over them in justice and peace. How could Jesus be the Messiah? Clearly, if the Messiah is Jesus, the meaning of "Messiah" had to be changed. This is precisely what the early believers did. Ever since, Christian understanding of Messiahship differs from that of the Jews.

The earliest Christians reread the Scriptures and found passages which pointed to an understanding of messiahship which included suffering (such as Isa. 53). Already the tradition which Paul learned (see p. 22) asserted that the Messiah "died for our sins in accordance with the scriptures" (1 Cor. 15:3), though it is not said which passages say this. Likewise, according to Acts, Peter asserted that "what God foretold by the mouth of all the prophets, that his Christ [the Messiah] should suffer, he thus fulfilled" (Acts 3:18).

Thus the first believers reinterpreted the Old Testament in order to show that Jesus' suffering was precisely what qualified him to be the Messiah, and that his resurrection proved it. So his resurrection too was argued on the basis of Scripture; in Acts 2:29-36 Peter argues that what is said in Psalms 16:8-11 and Psalms 110:1 applies only to Jesus. Such argumentation might appear strange to us, and less than persuasive. But in that context, this way of arguing from Scripture was accepted and expected. It is important to see that each in their own way—the people of the Dead Sea Scrolls, the Pharisees, the Sadducees, and the Christians—were convinced that it was they who rightly interpreted the Scriptures.

Those who accepted the message were called upon to repent—to change their ways and understanding of God's future and to commit themselves to Jesus. Those who did were baptized. We do not know how the earliest church interpreted baptism—probably as a sign of repentance and of entry into the true Israel. In any case, the function of baptism was to identify a new community, and thereby distinguish these people from everyone else.

That this community was a sect is clear from the fact that it regarded itself as the true Israel (for the meaning of "sect" see p. 13). A detail in the old tradition which Paul learned shows this clearly, for it says that the resurrected Christ appeared to "the twelve" (1 Cor. 15:5). Since Judas had committed suicide (Matt. 27:3-10), and since his successor had not yet been chosen (Acts 1:15-26), there were only "the eleven." But because "twelve" symbolized the whole people of Israel (the Twelve Tribes), the tradition spoke of "the twelve" in order to make a theological claim. Although ten of the traditional tribes had disappeared seven centuries earlier, it was part of Jewish hope that in God's new future the whole people of Israel would be reconstituted.

However, the Jesus-people were not the only ones who understood themselves in terms of "twelve." At Qumran there was a council of twelve elders because this commune also claimed to be the true Israel of the future. In other words, we call both the people at Qumran and the earliest Christians "sects" because both made exclusive claims to represent the true Israel of the New Age.

Now we can understand why the church would have handed on a saying of Jesus which promised the twelve disciples that they would sit on twelve thrones judging (ruling) the twelve tribes of Israel (Matt. 19:28, Luke 22:29-31). We also understand why they felt it necessary to replace Judas (Acts 1:15-26).

Although both the Jesus-people and the Qumranites can be called sects, they were quite different. Those who went to Qumran believed that only in the desert, away from all the contaminating influences of society, could they be the holy remnant prepared for the End. Those who joined adopted a strict discipline. Each new member was on probation for two years before being fully admitted; each member was assigned a rank as in an army. The believers in Messiah Jesus, on the other hand, did not withdraw into a convential but remained in society and actively sought converts. Nor was there a probationary period or assigned rank.

It is helpful to compare the Qumranites and the early church also with regard to their common life. Both were close-knit communities, as one expects in sects; both had common meals and shared property. At Qumran, it appears that new members were required to deposit their belongings with the community. They lived together and farmed communally owned land. The early church, however, does not appear to have required sharing wealth.

Our information is unfortunately very meager. All we know about the practice is two particular cases (a negative example in Acts 5:1-11, and a positive one in 4:36-37), and the generalizations of the author of Acts (Acts 2:44-46; 4:32, 34-35), who was describing it fifty years later. Not surprisingly, his generalizations are not altogether clear. In Acts 2:44; 4:32 he implies that everyone pooled his wealth but then he keeps pointing out that the money was distributed to the needy. Moreover, the group kept on meeting in private homes. Evidently some believers did sell their goods and put the money into a common fund for the needy. There is no reason to think that they pooled their capital in order to generate new wealth in common, as was done at Qumran; it was, rather, a consumer's commune, not a producers' co-op.

We do not know how the practice originated. There is no evidence that Jesus had required it. Nor do we know how long it was continued. It seems not to have spread to other centers of Christianity, though the custom of having common meals did. In any case, the new group manifested mutuality and concern for the well-being of everyone. Besides, if the Messiah was to come momentarily, and if then all things would be changed, what was the point of holding on to one's private possessions?

Another detail helps us to fill in the picture. According to Acts 9:43 Peter lived in the house of Simon, a tanner. According to Jewish customs, especially as nurtured by the Pharisees, tanners were regarded as outcasts because they worked with all sorts of hides and used urine in the leather-making process. They were regarded as ritually unclean.

But the young church was bent upon constituting the true Israel and so was unafraid to break down whatever barriers had kept Jews apart heretofore. Thus we read that various Jews joined the movement, including priests (Acts 6:7) and Pharisees (Acts 15: 5). Indeed, as the story of Acts proceeds, it is clear that some of the believers had no scruples at all about whom they invited to the Way, and that this generosity created one of the crises of the earliest church. In the next section we shall see who these believers were.

The Way of Stephen

Acts reports the spread of the gospel in a schematic way. First to be reached were the Aramaic-speaking Jews, then the Hellenized Jews (called "Hellenists" in Acts 6:1-8). It was the Hellenized Jews who became refugees from persecution in Jerusalem, and who spread the faith as they fled: first the Samaritans (Acts 8:4-25), then a gentile who could not have become a convert to Judaism because he had been castrated (Acts 8:26-40), then Hellenized Jews outside Palestine (Acts 11:19), and finally Greek pagans in Antioch (Acts 11:20, where "Hellenists" means "Greeks" as the RSV has it). For the author of Acts, the Hellenized Jews were the bridge between the Jerusalem church and the gentile world. As we saw in chapter 1 (see p. 16), he was right.

The leader of the Hellenized Jews in Jerusalem who believed the gospel was Stephen. Everything we know about him must be learned from Acts 6-7. The Book of Acts emphasizes that the first church was harmonious and regards the reports of sharing the wealth as the manifestation of this unity (see, e.g., Acts 4:32). In this light, it comes as a shock that Acts 6:1 introduces the Hellenists as grumblers. They were complaining that their widows were not getting a fair share of what was being distributed.

What was behind this discrimination? Evidently, the Aramaic-speaking Jews (here called "the Hebrews") showed a certain clannishness. Obviously it was not simply a matter of language because the Hellenized Jews were bilingual. Rather, the Hellenized Jews represented a different type of Judaism, perhaps a different social and economic level as well, and in any case were used to living more or less as Greeks. In other words, accepting these Jews into the true Israel did not automatically erase social distinctions and ingrained attitudes. Believing in Jesus and receiving the Spirit did not erase prejudice over night.

The solution, as reported by Acts, is nothing short of remarkable. The apostles made those who felt cheated responsible for the whole welfare program! The seven who were chosen have come to known as deacons (literally, servers), though they are not called this here. That they were all Hellenized Jews is clear from their names. We hear nothing more of them, except Stephen.

Nothing is said about Stephen administering the food distribution; instead, we read that he worked miracles as did the apostles (Acts 6:8; see 3:1-10; 5:12-16). Moreover, he evangelized other Hellenized Jews (Acts 6:7), evidently with some success. In other words, Stephen did what the apostles did and so must be viewed as a leader of a type of Christianity that was emerging among Hellenized Jews. This is confirmed by the fact that the first persecution left the apostles alone but was apparently directed at the Hellenists (Philip is a Greek name; Acts 8:4). Evidently the authorities were able to distinguish one kind of Christian from another, and to decide that the apostles were not as dangerous as the Hellenists.

The clearest evidence that the Hellenized Jews were developing a somewhat different kind of Christianity is found in their attitude toward the temple. The Aramaic-speaking Jews continued to regard it as God's sanctuary (Acts 5:42). But Stephen was accused of preaching against it and the law as well. Acts says this was a false charge (Acts 6:12-14), yet goes on to report that Stephen's speech actually confirmed the accusation (see Acts 7:44-50). To be sure, the speech is not a transcript of Stephen's words. Christians would have had no records of it if any had been made, and the author of Acts did not hear it. Nonetheless, it may well reflect the memory of the kind of thing Stephen had been saying before he became the first Christian martyr.

If Stephen spoke for the group, then it seems that the Hellenized Jews who believed in Jesus had little interest in the temple. The assertion that God does not live in man-made houses (Acts 7:48) is common among the Stoic philosophers, and Acts 17:24-25, where Paul speaks like a Stoic, makes the same point. But to mini-

33

mize the temple is to down-grade the one religious institution which embodied the nation as a religious entity; Jews in the diaspora sent money to it every year.

In other words, Stephen's circle had been sufficiently Hellenized to seek the spiritual meaning of Judaism and to play down its national institutional aspect without giving it up completely. When they came to believe in Jesus, they emphasized the spiritual meaning of doing so and saw no reason to start being concerned with the temple. Is it surprising that it was precisely these Jews who had no hesitation in sharing the gospel with Samaritans (who were hated by the Jews as apostates for having their own temple), with a eunuch (Acts 8:26-39), and finally with gentiles as well (Acts 11:19-20)?

Almost from the beginning, there emerged two kinds of Christianity within Jerusalem itself. The distinctive attitude of the Hellenists comes all the more clear when we look at an opposite development which emerged, apparently after Stephen was dead.

The Way of James

James had not been among those who followed his brother, Jesus, during his lifetime. As in Paul's case, it took a vision of the resurrected Lord to make him part of the Messiah's people (1 Cor. 15:7-8). Precisely when this occurred is not known; he is not mentioned in the list of the earliest circle given in Acts 1:12-14, and was not one of the nominees to replace Judas. Nonetheless, he came to be the leader in Jerusalem.

The original leader, however, was Peter. This is simply taken for granted in the early chapters of Acts. More important, the old tradition in 1 Corinthians 15, to which we have appealed often, says that the risen Lord appeared to "Cephas," not to "Simon," his real name. Cephas is the way *Kepha* was spelled in Greek, and the word mean Rock. "Peter," on the other hand, is the English for *Petros,* which translates the word into Greek. How Simon came to be known as Rock is reported in Matthew 16:13-19. Paul frequently refers to him this way (1 Cor. 1:12; 9:5; Gal. 1:18; 2:11). Thus the preeminence of Peter was recognized widely in early Christianity.

Nothing certain is known about how James came to be the leader in Jerusalem. However, it is quite possible that James came into this role because he represented a type of Christianity which was respected by non-believing Jews. What we know about James and this type of Christianity depends mostly on later Christian literature. One interesting tradition was recorded in the second

34

century, but we have it only in a quotation by Eusebius, a fourth century historian of Christianity. Here it is said that James

> . . . was holy from his mother's womb. He drank no wine or strong drink, nor did he eat meat; he put no razor on his head; he did not anoint himself with oil and he did not go to the baths. He alone was permitted to enter into the sanctuary for he did not wear wool but linen, and he used to enter alone into the temple and be found kneeling and praying for forgiveness for the people, so that his knees grew hard like a camel's.
> —Ecclesiastical History, II, 23:4-6.

According to the same account, James was clubbed to death after having been thrown off the wall of the temple. The story adds that the Roman siege of Jerusalem was God's punishment for his martyrdom.

This is clearly a legend, not a factual report. Still, it tells a good deal about how he was remembered, and this reveals important things about those who did the remembering. (In the same way, the legend of young George Washington confessing to having chopped down the cherry tree tells us about what early nineteenth century Americans valued in their President: lifelong, incorruptible honesty.) What do these memories tell us about the Jewish Christians who revered James?

• He was remembered as a Nazirite. The Nazirites were a small sect within Judaism who renounced civilization and modern ways in order to return to the old desert ideal. Nazirites were regarded as especially devout and holy persons. James himself probably was not a Nazirite; but his piety was such that he came to be regarded as a Christianized Nazirite. Obviously, those who viewed him this way also admired what he stood for in their eyes.

• He was remembered as one who was so holy that he could go where only the priests went, and who actually wore linen—the material worn by priests in the sanctuary. It is highly unlikely that James was allowed to function as a priest because this was a privilege one inherited from his father; no one could be "called to the priesthood" or volunteer for it. But those Jewish Christians who remembered James this way clearly valued the temple much more than did Stephen.

• James' reputation for praying on behalf of his people shows that those who admired him continued to see themselves inseparably bound up with the nation. They sensed no alienation from Judaism because of their faith in Jesus. In fact, being the Messiah's people made them even more loyal to the Jewish people, and hence to the law of Moses as well.

To be sure, these traditions are from a later time; but they are supported by what Acts reports that James said to Paul when he arrived in Jerusalem in the late 50's. Clearly the Jerusalem church does not know what to do with Paul:

> You see, brother, how many thousands there are among the Jews of those who have believed; they are all zealous for the law, and they have been told about you that you teach all the Jews who are among the Gentiles to forsake Moses. . . . What then is to be done?
>
> —Acts 21:20-22.

James came to represent a type of Christianity which was intensely devoted to temple and Torah. Believing in Messiah Jesus made these Jews doubly loyal to Judaism. It was but natural that they believed the rumor that Paul made renegade Jews out of those who accepted the gospel.

How, then, did this type of Christianity emerge as typical of Jerusalem? In the first place, the leader of the alternative view, Stephen, was dead and other leading Hellenists had left. Apparently the Christianity of the Hellenized Jews in Jerusalem faded out. In the next place, Acts hints that after Peter had been released from prison under marvellous circumstances, he left the city, either in order to evangelize elsewhere or in order to avoid endangering the church further (Acts 12:17). In Peter's absence James became the leader, and his kind of Christianity became representative. This could exist free from harassment among Jews who, under increasing Roman provocation, were ever more conscious of their Jewishness.

Even though much remains obscure about these two types of Christianity, it is clear that increasingly those of the Way had to face the question, Must the true Israel distinguish itself from Judaism and its concern for temple and Torah, or must it intensify its Jewishness? The rest of this chapter will explore some of the points where this issue came into focus.

THE TORAH IN THE YOUNG CHURCH

The Gospels as Clues to the Christians

We are accustomed to reading the Gospels to learn about Jesus. This time, however, we shall look at them to learn about the early Christians. To understand this procedure, we need to take account of the nature of the Gospels, especially the Synoptics (the first three).

First, the oldest Gospel is Mark, written around A.D. 70. Between Mark and Jesus there is a period of about forty years. Mark did not write down his personal memories of Jesus, since he was not an original disciple. Also, it is doubtful that he wrote the memories of Peter, as a second century writer claimed. Where then did he get his information? From a supply of sayings and stories about Jesus which were circulating in the churches, some of which had already been collected.

Between the time of Jesus and the written accounts of his ministry, sayings and stories about him circulated by word of mouth (what scholars call "the oral tradition"). Originally each item was told by itself as an independent piece of tradition. The oldest running account of Jesus' work was provided by Mark. Later, Matthew and Luke used Mark, as well as other material. This means that the Gospel of Mark reflects three distinct stages: the situation of Jesus, the period when the material circulated orally, and Mark's own situation for which he wrote.

Second, the Gospels clearly do not tell us everything Jesus said and did, and perhaps do not record everything that was circulating by word of mouth. What had been circulating was what Christians found important. Just as what was told about James revealed something about those who revered him, so what was handed on about Jesus discloses some things about the people who used this material.

Third, virtually all the material with which we are concerned here reports controversies between Jesus and the Pharisees. Usually it is critical of Jewish practices or else reports the Pharisees' criticism of the disciples. Almost nothing is said about agreements. Is this because they agreed on nothing but were bitter opponents at every point? Not at all. The early church did not try to preserve everything Jesus had said, or even a representative selection of it. Rather, they remembered those things which were useful in their own conflicts with Judaism, and perhaps with one another as well.

To guide them in these controversies, the early Christians relied on the traditions of what Jesus had said and done. The Gospel portrait of the Pharisees is one-sided because information about Jesus' agreements was not as important as that about his disagreements. This is why what they handed on about Jesus tells us about issues facing the Christians.

Fourth, in view of what we have already learned, two other things must not be forgotten. By the time the Gospels were written, Judaism had changed. The kind of Pharisee opposed by Matthew, for instance, is not identical with the Pharisees Jesus dealt

37

with. Also the stories of Jesus' conflicts with Pharisees probably were not handed on by the Christians who looked to James. They would have treasured memories of Jesus which showed him being obedient to the law. It is much more likely that the stories and sayings of Jesus' conflicts with the Pharisees were transmitted by the Hellenized Jewish Christians, like Stephen and his group. Later, of course, gentile Christians would have prized them. Marcion used them to argue that Jesus came to save us from Judaism altogether (see p. 8).

To summarize: the Synoptic Gospels reveal the problems of the people for whom these particular sayings and stories of Jesus were especially important. At the same time, one must not read later situations back into the time of Jesus.

What Must be Done on the Sabbath?

One community after another faces the question, What are we going to do about Sunday closing laws? As a matter of fact, how should Christians observe Sunday, whether or not stores are open? Today, many no longer understand why this is a religious question, and regard as quaint the stories older people tell about when it was a controversial matter. This reflects our history.

When Christians, especially those influenced by Calvinism, called Sunday "the Sabbath" they also applied the Old Testament Sabbath laws to Sunday. The dominant question was, What is one permitted to do? The question of how Christians are to observe the traditional day of rest is as old as Christianity.

The Sabbath was fundamental to Jewish life. Even outside Palestine, Jewish devotion to the Sabbath was respected by Roman law; emperors repeatedly confirmed the right of Jews to observe it according to their custom and exempted Jewish soldiers from bearing arms on the sacred day. To observe the day properly however, one had to make some decisions because the Old Testament was not specific enough (Exod. 20:11; 31:12-17; 35:1-3; Deut. 5:12-15). For example, Exodus 35:3 prohibits kindling fire, but can one use fire kindled just before the Sabbath began? Where there are no clocks, how does one tell precisely when the Sabbath begins and ends? (One answer: when one can no longer distinguish a white hair from a black one.) And what constitutes work?

The Pharisees undertook to answer such questions as precisely as possible so that everyone could know exactly what is expected. After A.D. 135 these definitions and legal rulings were compiled into a tract called "Sabbath," and included in an early code of laws called the Mishnah.

38

It is difficult to say how many of these rulings had been made before A.D. 70, or the extent to which they were actually put into practice even by the Pharisees. Some discussions appear to be academic exercises, as when law students argue cases in order to clarify legal points. Nonetheless, it is clear that the Pharisees (like the commune at Qumran) were deeply committed to scrupulous observance of the Sabbath, which they regarded as a privilege.

The Palestinian Jewish Christians continued to observe the Sabbath. True, Jesus' resurrection came to be celebrated on the first day of the week, also known as "the Lord's Day." Possibly the Jewish Christians assembled on Sunday and attended synagogue on Sabbath. Why not? They remembered that Jesus had attended it and taught there (Mark 2:18-22; 3:1; John 6:59). As we saw, many Jewish Christians continued to participate in Sabbath services in the synagogue until about A.D. 85.

Nonetheless, we conclude that some Jewish Christians developed a less scrupulous attitude toward Sabbath observance because they remembered stories in which Jesus' freer attitude was the controversial point. Except for the account of the disciples in the grain fields, they all concern Jesus' freedom to heal on the Sabbath.

Consider, for example, the story of the disciples in the fields. We shall look at it in some detail because it teaches us so much about the early Christian use of the Jesus-traditions. The story is found in Mark 2:23-28; Matthew expanded it into the form found in Matthew 12:1-8, while Luke's version is in Luke 6:1-5.

First, we note the various ways in which the story is told. Matthew and Luke made only minor changes when they copied Mark as far as Mark 2:26. But then both Matthew and Luke left out Mark 2:27: "and he said to them, 'and the Sabbath was made for man, not man for the Sabbath.'" (Some manuscripts of Mark also omit it.) Only Matthew adds the saying in Matthew 12:5-7. One important manuscript of Luke ends the story at Luke 6:4, and replaces the saying in verse 5 ("the Son of Man is Lord of the Sabbath") with a story: "On the same day, seeing someone working on the Sabbath, he said to him, 'Man, if indeed you know what you are doing, you are blessed; but if you do not know, you are cursed and a transgressor of the law.'"[1] Scholars are divided over whether this is a genuine saying of Jesus or not.

Second, in the oldest version (Mark) there are really three answers to the question, "Why are they doing what is not lawful

---

[1]From *Gospel Parallels,* Ed. Burton H. Throckmorton, Jr. Thomas Nelson, Inc., 1973, p. 51.

on the Sabbath?" Mark 2:25-26 appeals to the precedent of David (1 Sam. 21:1-7): If David can do what is illegal when there was human need, then the disciples can do so too. Mark 2:27 argues that "the Sabbath was made for man, not man for the Sabbath"—something which Pharisees also believed. They did not, however, use this point to justify a lax attitude toward Sabbath laws. Mark 2:28 asserts that the Son of Man (assumed to be Jesus) is Lord even of the Sabbath, as if he had authority to permit the disciples to violate the Sabbath law, and as if he had done so.

Each of these three answers can stand on its own; there is no clear logical connection between them. This shows that Mark's account compiles three answers to the question. This is confirmed by the fact that verse 27 begins all over again with "and he said to them." Actually, verse 27 was probably the original answer; verses 25-26 were inserted later, just as verse 28 was added.

Third, all versions of the story assume that the Sabbath is to be observed; nothing is said about replacing Sabbath with Sunday. That will come later, and not in Palestine but in the Greek churches. Each version is concerned with giving reasons why Christians are not scrupulous about Sabbath observance, why they observe it with a measure of freedom which the Pharisees found objectionable. It is also possible that the story reflects arguments *within* the Christian communities over proper Sabbath observance. Conceivably, those Christians who looked to James would have been as scrupulous about the Sabbath as the Pharisees, while the Hellenistic Jewish Christians would have had a more liberal attitude. Perhaps our story reflects arguments between these groups.

Fourth, by combining what we have learned about the stages of the story as it stands in Mark with how Mark's account was used later, we can trace the development of early Christian thinking about Sabbath observance.

• Clearly, Christians did not remember this story because they too were in the habit of picking ears of grain on the Sabbath. Rather, they used this story as a precedent or warrant for their own freer attitude. Perhaps they had less hesitation about cooking on the Sabbath, or walking beyond the specified distance which was permitted. If questioned by their neighbors about their relative indifference to certain aspects of Sabbath observance, they could have answered by repeating the original story (Mk. 2:23-24, 27) which ended with "The Sabbath was made for man, not man for the Sabbath."

• Since this was not a new idea in Judaism, Christians faced the question of why they concluded that this gave them the right to ignore the Sabbath laws. The second stage of the story reflects their answer: "The Son of Man is Lord even of the Sabbath." That is, in the name of Jesus' authority they are free to observe the Sabbath as they do.

• But does this not imply that Jesus is at odds with the scripture which commands Sabbath observance? Not at all, for the Bible itself reports times when the command was broken. Thus the third stage (Mk. 2:25-26) appeals to what David himself did. The logic of this appeal is not quite clear. According to some Jewish traditions, however, David ate the holy bread on a Sabbath. If those who added Mark 2:25-26 knew that tradition, they would be reasoning, "Look, even David violated the Sabbath and you do not accuse him."

On the other hand, nothing is actually said about David doing this on the Sabbath. What is said is that David and his associates were hungry. This implies that in time of human need one can disregard the Sabbath regulations. This also agrees with the point in verse 27: The Sabbath is for human good and Sabbath observance must not interfere with it.

• However, Mark did not actually say that the disciples were hungry. Matthew saw this and added this detail in 12:1 in order to make the logic of the appeal to David clear. (Matthew also, like Luke, dropped Mark's reference to Abiathar the high priest because this is not correct; some manuscripts of Mark also leave it out.)

Matthew is not content to say that in time of need one can violate the Sabbath law. By adding Matthew 12:5-6 he argues that the disciples are not guilty at all. On the one hand, Matthew 12:5-6 points out that on the Sabbath the priests carry out their duties and are not guilty of breaking the law. Since Jesus is greater than the temple, being faithful to Jesus also does not make one guilty. On the other hand, the quotation of Hosea 6:6 ("I [God] desire mercy and not sacrifice") implies that God does not require scrupulous observance in the first place.

Other stories were remembered because they showed Jesus' freedom to heal on the Sabbath.

• Luke 13:10-17 reports that Jesus healed a woman who had been unable to stand erect for eighteen years. The objection (vs. 14) expressed the view of the Pharisees—where life is in danger one is permitted to heal on the Sabbath. Otherwise, one must wait. The woman's life was clearly not in danger; besides, after almost twenty years she could surely wait one more day. But not Jesus. His reply is an indirect argument: on the Sabbath you untie your animals in order to water them (so they may live); on the Sab-

41

bath, can you not release a person from Satan so she may live? After all, he implies, a person is more than an animal. He simply assumes that her condition is caused by Satan.

• According to Luke 14:1-6 Jesus took the initiative in posing the issue and then answered his own question by healing the man. Again, Jesus justified his action by appealing to what was legal in the case of an animal. This saying must have circulated independently at one time because in Matthew 12:9-14 it is used in connection with an altogether different story.

• Mark 3:1-6 also reports that Jesus seized the initiative in putting the issue and then deliberately healed the man's hand to make his point. In using Mark, however, Matthew made two interesting changes. He no longer has Jesus taking the initiative, but has him responding to a question which his critics put to him (Matt. 12:9-10). Also, he inserted the saying about rescuing an animal (this time a sheep), and then has Jesus make the argument explicit.

• According to Jerome, a fifth century biblical scholar, the Gospel of the Hebrews added a detail to the story of the man with the withered hand. (This Gospel is known to us only in scattered quotations in later Christian literature; evidently it was used by Jewish Christians.) Here, the man asked for help: "I was a mason, seeking a living with my hands; and I beg you, Jesus, restore my health to me, so that I need not beg for my food in shame." Adding this makes it clear that Jesus was responding to a particular case, not illustrating a general principle. In other words, the Jewish Christians who used this version of the story weakened the freedom with which Jesus acted; what Jesus did was really an exception.

Taking these stories as a whole, we see that (apart from the Gospel of the Hebrews) they were not remembered because Christians were interested in healing on the Sabbath (though they may have done so), but because they illustrate the principle that whatever promotes human good is as permissible on the Sabbath as on any other day. But this is the wrong way to put it. Actually, what must be done—that which is for the good of persons—must be done on the Sabbath too; it is as mandatory then as on the next day. However, the Gospel of the Hebrews guards against just this use of the story.

It is ironic that centuries later, especially in English and North American Puritanism, Sunday came to be observed with the sort of rigidity which some early Chritsians had sought to overcome. Today, of course, we face an entirely different set of problems arising from a five-day work week (or less), long weekends, the acceptance of recreation as a necessity, and days off staggered so as not to interrupt industry or transportation. If in working out our own attitudes toward Sunday we appeal to these stories, we do the same sort of thing which the early Christians did. It is interesting to ask, however: With which of these Gospels do we find the greater kinship?

What Defiles a Person?

It is difficult for Protestants to appreciate how important for Judaism were (and still are) kosher food laws, as well as other regulations regarding "clean and unclean" things. Jews were not the only people who had such customs and taboos. We need to remember that "clean" and "unclean" does not refer to sanitary cleanliness but to religious purity before God. Whatever is "unclean" contaminates, pollutes, or defiles a person, and thereby hampers one's relation to God.

Certain things were therefore taboo, such as certain foods (e.g., pork, shellfish), graves and corpses, and menstruating women. Moreover, "uncleanness" is contagious; it can be transmitted indirectly, as when a person touches a dish or a tool which had previously touched an unclean object or person. Since contact with defiling things and/or persons was often inevitable, it was possible to remove the "uncleanness" by ritual washing and other rites. It was better, of course, to avoid becoming "unclean"; this required knowing what did and did not have defiling power. Understandably, laws concerning food had to be carefully worked out.

For Jews, maintaining the laws of purity was also an important way of preserving national identity. We do not know, of course, how many of the regulations now found in the Mishnah had been worked out before A.D. 70, nor how widely observed if they were. Still, the laws about "clean" and "unclean" food were a basic part of Jewish culture.

Christianized Jews took it for granted that believing in Jesus did not cancel the obligation to observe these laws. This is shown in the story of how Peter came to go to Cornelius, the Roman officer (Acts 10). While Peter was waiting for lunch, he had a vision in which he saw a sheet come down from heaven; in it were all kinds of animals, reptiles, and birds. When a voice asked him to eat some of this, he replied, "No, Lord; for I have never eaten anything that is common or unclean."

The point of the vision, of course, is that God has declared Cornelius to be "clean" because he was a devout man. Only if the food laws were being observed could such a vision occur, or a report of it carry any weight, or cause Peter to be criticized,

43

"Why did you go to an uncircumcized man and eat with him?" (Acts 11:3).

These considerations make it all the more remarkable that the saying of Jesus in Mark 7:15 was preserved: "There is nothing outside a man which by going into him can defile him; but things which come out of a man are what defile him." This saying is now part of a long passage dealing with Jewish law. All of it is important for our topic, though we can discuss only what pertains to food.

The passage (Mk. 7:1-23) compiles various sayings that are critical of Jewish tradition. We need to distinguish individual elements. The story begins by raising the issue of eating without washing hands—that is, without taking care of defilement which might have been incurred. But the question in verse 5 is not answered until verse 15. In between stand two other sayings which have nothing to do with the question about defilement (Mk. 7: 6-13). They deal with the oral tradition.

In order to pick up the question, as well as to address the answer to everyone, the compiler revised verse 14. (Some important manuscripts do not have v. 16; the RSV has it in a footnote.) Mark 7:17-23 gives an explanation of Jesus' reply in verse 15. We also detect statements which explain things to the reader (vv. 3-4 and the last part of v. 19); the RSV puts these into parentheses. They were added later, probably by Mark himself, for no one in Palestine before A.D. 70 would need to have these things explained.

The old Palestinian story concerned defilement by food and probably consisted of Mark 7:1-2, 5, an early form of verse 14, and verse 15. Jesus' reply to the question in verse 5 compresses a complicated response into a deceptively simple statement. It is in fact a riddle in two parts, neither of which by itself answers the question. Taken together they respond to a position hidden in the question asked. We need to retrace the logic built into this early story.

The question in verse 5 assumes that if the hands are not washed ritually defilement enters the person as he or she eats and so bars access to God. The questioners want to know, therefore, why Jesus' followers are not concerned about this danger. If the answer had consisted only of the first part (nothing outside can defile a person by entering him), it would be incomplete because one would not know what it is that does defile, only what does not. Had the answer consisted only of the second part (what comes out is what defiles), it would have been incomplete because it would not answer the question. Also it would be banal because

44

everybody knew that things which come out defile (puss, excrement, menstrual blood).

So long as one thinks of defilement as something that is transmitted physically, even the two parts together do not make sense. The answer makes sense only if the second part is understood in a new way, metaphorically. But this implies a new understanding of defilement, and with it goes a different list of "what comes out." Thus Jesus' reply in verse 15 is a riddle—a saying which calls for insight before it is understood. How did Christians come to understand it?

In verse 17 Mark introduces the explanatory verses with his typical editorial device—private explanation of public teaching. (He did this also in Mk. 4:10 and 13:1-4; Matthew and Luke felt free to change these accents on private instruction.) The explanation itself consists of two parts. Verses 18-19 explain why what goes in cannot defile—it enters only the stomach and then is evacuated. Therefore it does not reach the real self, the heart where decisions are made. Verses 20-23 explain what comes out of a person which does defile. These things are not physical at all but moral. To make this clear there follows a list of vices. Some of these words have no Aramaic equivalent, showing that the list was developed by Greek-speaking Christians.

What does this analysis show us? First, some early Christians concluded that the force of Jesus words was that food laws no longer matter at all—as verse 19 puts it, "he declared all foods clean." The story did not report that Jesus actually made such a ruling; he did not answer the question, May one eat pork or crabmeat? His concern had been with the right understanding of defilement. Nonetheless, some Christians concluded that if nothing defiles a person by going into the mouth, then it does not matter what one eats. This conclusion must have been reached by gentile Christians. Here we see how early Christians used the tradition of Jesus' teaching to deal with problems in their own situation.

Second, Matthew left out precisely the general principle in Mark 7:19, and concluded the teaching by reminding the reader that the whole discussion has to do with unwashed hands (Matt. 15:1-20). Since Matthew was using Mark, leaving out Mark 7:19 shows that he disagreed with Mark's understanding of Jesus' teaching. Matthew was too close to Jewish Christians to draw the conclusion that Jesus abolished food laws, even implicitly. (Luke left out this part of Mark altogether.) In other words, Matthew shows a disagreement over the meaning of Jesus' teaching.

Third, it is worth asking whether Christians today are closer to Matthew than to Mark when the subject of food and drink comes up.

CHRISTIANS AND THE LIBERATION OF ISRAEL

Possibly the most explosive issue for the early Palestinian Christians were the events that led to outright revolt against Rome. If Jesus is the *Messiah,* would not his coming in power crown the guerilla warfare with astounding success? On the other hand, if the Messiah is *Jesus,* does his coming in power really have anything to do with the guerilla freedom fighters? But then how could he be the Messiah, the expected liberator of Israel?

The Christians had to make up their minds whether to stand solidly with their fellow Jews or not. To refuse to become involved in the revolution was to risk being called apostates and traitors. But if they disengaged themselves, could they still claim to be the true Israel? Doubtless, such questions weighed heavily on the consciences of the Jewish Christians in Palestine.

The Silence of the New Testament

Surprisingly, however, apart from a few allusions the New Testament totally ignores the First Revolt against Rome in A.D. 66-70, the most important event in the history of Judaism between the destruction of the first temple in 586 B.C. and the creation of the modern state of Israel in 1948. To speak of the Palestinian Christians' attitude toward the Revolt we must rely largely on circumstantial evidence.

For one thing, it would have been difficult to remain aloof. We recall how many Christians, of all sorts and levels of commitment, were involved in the various resistance movements against the Nazis in World War II. They could not stand aside and become silent accomplices with the Germans against their own people. Would it have been easier in Graeco-Roman Palestine?

Moreover, repeatedly the temple was the focal point of the controversy with Rome. Could one worship daily in the temple and not care about it? The logic of the situation argues that the Christians could not have been indifferent. The more compelling the logic, however, the more intriguing is the silence.

Is the silence accidental or deliberate? Some argue that the New Testament is deliberately silent because the writers suppressed the evidence in order to disassociate themselves from the Jewish Christians. Furthermore, it is claimed that also the picture of Jesus was retouched to conceal his sympathy with the revolutionary movement. Consequently, it is argued, the Gospels blame his crucifixion on the Jews and "whitewash" Pilate.

Even so, some authentic facts shine through. For example, Jesus was crucified with insurrectionists ("robber" is a misleading translation, it is claimed). The charge nailed to the cross was "King of the Jews"—a revolutionary title. It is also argued that Christians were actively involved in the revolt. Clearly, we cannot rehearse arguments, for or against, such conclusions. We are interested here in the attitude of the Palestinian Christians toward the revolution and what led up to it.

Tyranny and Resistance

The death of Herod in 4 B.C. marked the end of an era. Under Herod, the Jews had been somewhat independent of Rome; at least they did not have to pay tribute money to Rome nor did Roman troops occupy the country. But after Herod, Emperor Augustus annexed Judea and Samaria to the Roman province of Syria and appointed Procurators to rule in the name of the emperor and collect the tribute. They ruled from Caesarea, on the coast.

One of the first things that marked the new situation was the census taken by Quirinius in A.D. 6. The purpose of the census was to get official tax rolls for the tribute to Rome; understandably, Jews loathed it. In fact it produced a revolt led by a Galilean named Judas; it is mentioned in Acts 5:37. According to Josephus, Judas and his supporters argued that this census would lead to complete slavery, and they called upon the people to resist. They argued that even if they failed, they would at least have the honor of having died in a good cause. Moreover God would help them. But the revolt failed; however, the insurrectionist movement went underground to emerge later.

The Procurators were determined to impose Roman authority. They did so by controlling the office of the High Priest. The High Priesthood was supposed to be inherited and the term was for life. But one Procurator appointed four different persons within eleven years, the last being Caiaphas, who was High Priest during the trial of Jesus.

The High Priests, in other words, became front men for Rome. This alienated them from the lesser priests and from the poorer Jews generally, since the High Priests were also among the wealthy families. Nonetheless, except for those at Qumran, the people continued to attend the temple services, for the ritual was commanded by God even if the temple was currently in the hands of scoundrels.

47

The earlier Procurators respected Jewish abhorrence of idolatry. So they sent their troops to the garrison in Jerusalem without the emblems (the army standards or banners), which included images of the emperor. Since these emblems were also used in the religious ceremonies of the troops, the Jews regarded them as idols and insisted that they not be brought to Jerusalem. But one of the first things that Pilate did, when he arrived as Procurator in A.D. 26, was to order the troops to cover the emblems and take them to Jerusalem by night. One can easily imagine the Roman glee and the Jewish rage the next morning. A great crowd went to Caesarea to demonstrate for a week. Finally Pilate relented and ordered the emblems removed. Pilate later infuriated the Jews by confiscating temple money to build an aquaduct.

It was a later emperor, however, who provoked a more serious crisis. In A.D. 38 Gaius (also known by his nickname, Caligula = "Little Boots") took revenge on the Jews because at the coastal town of Jamnia they had torn down an altar to himself. He ordered that a huge gold-gilded statue of Zeus (or of himself looking like Zeus?) be erected in the Jerusalem temple. The governor of Syria, who was to carry out the order, dallied. Crowds of Jews met him to protest and to warn of the dire consequences if he went ahead. Only the death of Gaius spared the outbreak of war in A.D. 40. When Galilee also was placed under the rule of the Procurators, in A.D. 44, the whole country had lost the last semblance of semi-autonomy.

From now on, it is hard to see how disaster could have been averted. A messianic leader named Theudas urged the Jews to follow him to the Jordan where he would part the waters—implying that he was a new Moses. The waters did not separate, and Theudas was beheaded. (Acts 5:36 mentions this incident, but for some reason puts it before the revolt of Judas the Galilean, which had occurred a generation earlier.) Soon after the Theudas incident, the emperor Claudius outraged the Jews by appointing an apostate Jew as Procurator, Tiberius Alexander. He, in turn, had two sons of Judas the Galilean crucified.

Tiberius Alexander was soon replaced by Cumanus (in A.D. 48). During his four-year term, turmoil increased. Once, during Passover, a Roman soldier made an obscene gesture at the pilgrims and a bloody riot followed. Another time, insurgents attacked the troops in Galilee. Revenge was swift: the troops were ordered to pillage the villages nearby. When a soldier burned a copy of the Torah, the Jews demanded that he be punished. Rather than provoke open revolt by refusing, Cumanus ordered him executed. Josephus reports that from now on the land was filled with "outlaws" (his word also means "revolutionary"). Rebel bands formed, often raiding the estates of the wealthy who were favorable to Rome.

Another messianic leader appeared, this time from Egypt; he assembled a crowd on the Mount of Olives where he promised that the walls of Jerusalem would tumble as the walls of Jericho had for Joshua. He too was quashed. This incident is mentioned in Acts 21:38. Given the turmoil, it is not surprising that Judea was behind in paying tribute to Rome, or that the Procurator made up the deficit by raiding the temple bank.

In A.D. 66, the Revolt itself broke out when the priests stopped the daily sacrifice for the well-being of the emperor—an act which symbolized the end of loyalty to Rome. At the same time, the revolutionaries seized the fortress of Masada near the Dead Sea. Civil war broke out in Jerusalem. Rebels burned the palaces of the aristocracy and the public archives where the records of debts were kept. Menahem, son of Judas the Galilean, assumed command and had the current High Priest executed. Menahem himself was murdered while at prayer in the temple.

Repeatedly, one faction fought another for supremacy among the revolutionaries. But all was in vain, for in A.D. 70 the siege of Jerusalem began. On August 29, the city fell. The temple was burned, and what earlier Jews had succeeded in forestalling now occurred. The Roman emblems were set up in the sacred areas and the victors sacrificed to them.

But in the mountains of Judea, rebels held out for three more years. At Qumran, the faithful hid their library in caves shortly before the community was destroyed in A.D. 68. These scrolls were not to be found until 1947. At last even Masada fell in A.D. 73; there were no prisoners, for the defenders had made a suicide pact. In recent years, fascinating materials have been found at Masada, putting us in direct touch with the defenders who said in effect, "Better dead than Roman."

Christian Responses to Revolution

One would scarcely guess from the Book of Acts that the early Christians lived in such tumultuous times, despite the occasional references to insurgents. The author was not interested in writing the history of Christianity in the modern sense. Besides, he ended the story before the war started.

According to a later report, the Christians fled Jerusalem before it fell and went to Pella, southeast of Galilee. Some Jewish Christian groups survived for another century or more and then disappeared. They were hostile to Paul and Greek Christianity; the

49

church, in turn, declared them to be heretics. How Christianity might have developed had there remained a strong Jewish church in Jerusalem is one of the things we shall never know.

To get a sense of the issues faced by the believers in Jesus during the years before the War, we must use the Gospels, as we did in the previous section.

We begin with the story of Jesus and the explosive issue of the tribute tax demanded by Rome (Mark 12:13-17). It was not a matter of paying taxes as we know them, for our taxes are used to finance our own governments. Rome assessed subject nations a certain sum as a sign of their submission. Nor was it a matter of paying the costs of the occupation army. Rather, Jews were required to enrich Rome. The money was raised by a tax, based on the census (see p. 47). It was not a theoretical question about "church and state" or about taxes in general which was put to Jesus, but one which symbolized the subjection of the people.

Jesus' reply to the question of the tribute tax is well-known: "Give Caesar's things to Caesar and God's things to God." Here we are interested in what the story might have meant to the Palestinian Christians. We limit ourselves to three observations.

First, Jesus asked to see a denarius, the coin with which the tax was to be paid. Zealots refused, apparently, to have anything to do with the coin. Later some rabbis refused even to look at a coin with the emperor's image on it since he claimed to be divine. The community which remembers that its Lord asks to look at the coin was not outraged by the mere sight of it.

Second, Jesus forced his questioners to acknowledge that the coin had Caesar's name and inscription ("Tiberius Caesar, august son of the august god"). Jesus implied, "It's his money; give it to him." Those who repeated the story could not have been unalterably hostile to paying the tax.

Third, the twofold reply is formulated in precisely parallel phrases: "Give to Caesar what is Caesar's, and (or, but) give to God what is God's." Caesar gets what bears his image, God gets what has his—namely humankind. When one gives God what is God's—namely oneself—then the tax is no longer so important.

By telling this story, Christians could remind themselves not to get too involved in the issue. It is not a matter of "what is lawful" (the way the question was put in vs. 14), but what is the right thing to do. Jesus avoided being trapped, by neither rejecting the tax as illegal nor commending it unequivocally. The community that held itself accountable to such a story was apparently struggling to find a middle way between outright collaboration with Rome and outright resistance.

One clue to the Palestinian Christian response to Gaius' order to have Zeus' statue placed in the temple is found in Mark 13, a rather difficult chapter. In some ways it reads like an apocalyptic tract. Pamphlets and books concerned with the coming of the end, the last judgment, the punishment of the wicked, and the new world are called "apocalyptic" because these writings claim to report what was revealed. The Greek word for "revelation" is *apokalypsis* as in the *Apokalypsis to John* (the Revelation to John).

The Bible contains many passages that express the apocalyptic point of view, but only two books are commonly called apocalypses —Daniel and Revelation. But the Judaism of the New Testament period produced many such writings, as did some of the early Christians.

Mark 13 is often called "the little Apocalypse." Many scholars are persuaded that here Jesus steps out of character, so to speak, because nowhere else in the Gospels does he speak quite as he does here. Consequently it is widely believed that Mark (or the tradition on which he relied) wove together some authentic sayings of Jesus with Jewish apocalyptic traditions. This would not have been difficult to do because Jesus' own preaching shared important perspectives with apocalyptic ideas. We need not pursue the question further because our immediate concern is not with Jesus' own thought but with what was handed on as having come from him.

Several items in this complicated chapter show us something of the Christian response to the times. First, they expect the temple to be destroyed (Mk. 13:2). Moreover, Mark 13:14 refers to "the desolating sacrilege." This phrase is taken from Daniel 11: 27, 31; 12:11 where it refers to the pagan altar which had been set up in the temple in 168 B.C. (see also 1 Maccabees 1:54, 59; 6:7). In other words, Christians used the language of Daniel to talk about the statue ordered by Gaius, for it was the same sort of threat. Note that Mark 13:14 seems to assume that the statue will actually stand there. (This would be clearer if the Greek did not change from speaking of a thing [neuter] to a person [masculine] in verse 14; the RSV obscures this by translating "*it* ought not to be" instead of "*he* ought not to be.")

What are the Christians to do? Fight for the recovery of the temple as did the Maccabees in 168 B.C.? No, it is doomed. They are to flee (Mk. 13:14-18). Perhaps the prophet who urged them to flee in A.D. 70 was inspired by our passage from an earlier decade. The general tone of the chapter shows that the command to flee to the hills is not an order to join the guerillas but to

51

abandon the city to its fate. Whoever hands down such material does not share the "better dead than Roman" mentality.

Second, however, the Christians did not reach such a mind without struggle; probably some of them were more deeply involved in the revolt than others. Mark 13:5, 21-22 seem to warn against being deceived by leaders who make messianic claims. Such warnings would not have been remembered had there been no need to do so. Did figures like Theudas make this warning necessary? Matthew 24:26, which has no equivalent in Mark, seems to have such figures in mind. It is easy, moreover, to see how families would be divided; those who demanded participation in the revolution would regard those who refused as traitors. Mark 13:9-13 reflects these conflicts, though the passage as it stands has been reworked to take account of a wider range of persecution experiences.

Finally, some Christians apparently were so caught up in expecting these events to mark the End of All Things that they had to be warned against miscalculation (Mk. 13:7, 32-37). These events do show that the end is near, but still it is not yet here. The purpose of Mark 13:24-27 is to make this plain, for some things must occur *after* the "tribulation" (an allusion to the apocalyptic idea that there will be a time of "messianic woes"): the collapse of cosmic order. Only after this will the Son of Man come.

In other words, the crisis in Judea was understood in an apocalyptic way. But at the same time, it proved necessary to warn against believing that the Son of Man would come at the height of this crisis. No one knows exactly when that will be (Mk. 13:32). It was necessary to insist that not even Jesus knew the exact time because some were claiming to know this. Had they not made such claims, why would Christians have reminded one another of what even Jesus did not know?

We have had to be selective and brief in our discussion of Jewish Christians in Palestine. The issues we touched were not theirs alone, of course. In fact, we shall meet some of them again in Antioch.

Chapter Three
CHRISTIANITY BECOMES COSMOPOLITAN

Christians have seldom agreed on many things. In fact, within twenty years they were disagreeing over whether it was enough to be a Christian—a person committed to Jesus as the Messiah (Christ). Today, people may ask if one must be a Christian in order to be saved because "Christian" seems too restrictive. Then, however, some regarded "Christian" as not restrictive enough and argued that one had to be a Jew as well. This position did not prevail, and Christianity became more and more a gentile religion. Today, we debate whether we ought to convert Jews to Christianity; then, they debated whether to admit gentiles without making them Jews at the same time.

The issue came to a head in the second major center of Christianity, Antioch in Syria. What sort of Christianity developed here?

We shall distinguish roughly three stages, or "generations." The first is often called "apostolic"—the time of the apostles (up to A.D. 70). The second is sometimes called "sub-apostolic"—not because it is of lower quality but because we "come down" in time to about A.D. 100. The third generation extends to about A.D. 130-140.

From the start, Antioch was cosmopolitan. The population consisted of various kinds of Greeks, retired soldiers, the local people, and Jews. It was founded as the capital city of the Seleucid kingdom (see p. 25). Like the new cities founded by Alexander the Great, it was a planned Greek city, with a grid system of streets, theaters, gymnasiums, religious shrines, shops in arcades, and public toilets downtown. Antiochus IV (175-63 B.C.) brought the city to such a new level of splendor that he was called "the second founder." (He was the persecutor of the Jews, the instigator of the Maccabean revolt; see p. 26.)

With the rise of Roman power, the successors of Antiochus IV declined in power and influence. In 64 B.C. Syria (of which Antioch was the capital) was annexed to the Roman empire. At the beginning of the Christian era, Antioch enjoyed the benefits of being the major center of Roman power in the East. Repeatedly, when eastern puppet kings visited the city, as did emperors from time to time, they added to the city's statues, theaters, and baths. Even Herod of Judea took pride in helping to beautify it during his frequent visits.

Antioch also became famous for its own Olympic games, which attracted wealthy patrons and thousands of visitors. Equally famous was its wealthy suburb, Daphne, noted for its religious shrine in a parklike setting. The general standard of living in Antioch appears to have been fairly high. Populations of ancient cities are difficult to estimate; at the beginning of the Christian era Antioch evidently had about 300,000 inhabitants, not counting slaves or children. By the fourth century, it had grown to almost half a million; about 12 percent were Jews throughout this era. In short, the Antioch in which Christianity developed was a thriving cosmopolitan city, important for government, trade, sports, education, and religion.

The Jewish community was one of the largest outside Palestine, though not as large as that in Alexandria. Jews lived in their own sections of the city, much as national groups today tend to cluster together in Chicago or Boston. The Jewish quarter was not a ghetto, for Jews were not confined to it. They had certain civic rights, which included the right to develop their own schools, synagogues, courts and professional societies. Generally, Jews were free to participate broadly in the life and commerce of the city. Apparently there were three Jewish quarters in Antioch.

From time to time the Antiochene Jews endured anti-Jewish harassment and even persecution. When Gaius ordered the statue placed in the Jerusalem temple (see p. 48), they joined the delegation from Jerusalem to protest the action to the governor. This led to civil disturbances. According to Josephus, in the years immediately before the revolt in Palestine there was widespread animosity against Jews in Syria, but not in Antioch. But when the war broke out, anti-Jewish demonstrations arose there also.

Toward the end of the war, the Jews were blamed for a great fire, largely because a Jewish official said (falsely) that Jews had plotted to burn the city. When the conqueror of Jerusalem, Titus, returned to Antioch he was asked to expel all Jews, but he refused. Apparently during the first forty years of the Christian era the Jewish community in Antioch enjoyed stability.

54

In a large cosmopolitan city like Antioch, it is likely that there was considerable diversity among both the Jewish synagogues and the newly-formed Christian house churches—the small congregations of Christians who met in homes. Such groups doubtless consisted of the host household and its friends, relatives, and certain neighbors. (It would be a long time before Christians would meet in church buildings.) It was easy for each house church to develop its own style, habits of worship, and emphasis in teaching.

APOSTOLIC CHRISTIANITY IN ANTIOCH

We can learn about the first-generation Christians there from a firsthand account by Paul (in his letter to the Galatians, to be discussed more fully in chap. 5) and a secondhand account in Acts from the end of the next generation. Even though Acts was not written in Antioch, it used old memories circulating there about the early days. Unfortunately, much that we would like to know is not reported by either Paul or Acts, and some of what they do say does not agree. Consequently, every attempt to tell the story has its problems.

More than a Transplant

Right from the start, Christianity in Antioch had innovative impulses. According to Acts, it was the Hellenized Jewish Christian refugees from Jerusalem who brought the gospel to the capital city (Acts 11:19-20; see p. 33). They may not have realized how momentous was the decision to share the Good News also with Greeks. (In Acts 11:20 the word "Hellenists" means "Greeks," not Hellenized Jews as it does in Acts 6:1.) Since these Hellenized Jews from Jerusalem had long ago adopted Greek ways they apparently saw no reason why Greeks and other gentiles should be excluded. As a result, there came into existence the first "interracial" church. How many of the house churches consisted of only Jews or only of gentiles, and how many included both, we do not know.

When news of this development reached Jerusalem, the church dispatched a Jew from Cyprus—Barnabas—to see that things were developing properly. He liked what he saw, and left for Tarsus to fetch Saul/Paul. For a year they guided this exciting new venture (Acts 11:22-26).

Saul/Paul had been actively persecuting the church before his conversion, and when he himself became a refugee and arrived in Jerusalem it was Barnabas who vouched for the genuineness of his conversion. After he had to flee again, he returned to Tarsus,

55

in southeastern Asia Minor (Acts 8:1-3; 9:1-30). Here Barnabas found him and persuaded him to come to Antioch. Whereas the Jerusalem church became ever more loyal to Judaism, especially after Peter left (see chapter 2), these two figures guided the Antioch church into becoming the center of a Christianity that included gentiles, Hellenized Jews, and doubtless traditional Jews as well.

It was here, says Acts 11:26, that the name "Christians" was first used. The word must have been coined later, however, because Paul never uses it. Evidently it was invented by outsiders, like Quaker or Methodist. This name shows that "Christ" was regarded almost as a proper name, not as a title (Messiah).

Acts reports that this church sent a relief mission to Jerusalem during hard times (Acts 11:27-30). The story is easy to understand; it is what Paul says in Galatians 1:15-24 that creates difficulties.

Paul insists that after his conversion he did not go to Jerusalem but to Arabia (the Syrian desert), and then back to Damascus. Acts says nothing about a trip to Arabia but says he went to Jerusalem, and from there to Tarsus (Acts 9:26-30). Paul says that three years after his conversion he did go to Jerusalem and from there to Syria and Cilicia (the area of Tarsus). Is this visit to Jerusalem the same one which Acts reports? Apparently not, because Acts implies an extended stay, public preaching, and associating with the Apostles. Paul, however, insists that he stayed but two weeks and saw only Cephas (Peter) and James.

Paul says nothing about the relief mission, but according to Acts Paul and Barnabas took the money to Jerusalem. In fact, Paul denies that, apart from the two-week visit, he went to Jerusalem until fourteen years after his conversion. Since he is recounting all his relationships to Jerusalem, it is unlikely that he would have forgotten the relief visit.

All sorts of suggestions have been made to solve these problems, and none of them is fully satisfactory. Where does this leave us? Historians insist that we must follow Paul because he is reporting his own career, and is virtually taking an oath that his account is accurate (Gal. 1:20). Acts, on the other hand, was written forty years after these events and must rely on memories in the Antiochene community.

The only real problem is whether Paul was in the delegation that took the money to Jerusalem. Common memory could easily have come to report that he had done so since he had been an important figure in the Antioch church during the early years. We shall therefore see what the Antiochene memory reveals apart from the reference to Paul.

First, it was remembered that a Jerusalem prophet named Agabus appeared in Antioch. He must have been a rather well-known wandering prophet, for in Acts 21:10 he was in Caesarea to warn Paul not to go to Jerusalem. The early church had many such holy persons (women included, according to Acts 21:8-9) who were believed to be able to predict the future. They customarily moved from place to place, accepting Christian hospitality.

Second, in taking Agabus seriously, the Antioch church was open to apocalyptic predictions, for world-wide famine was one of the things often predicted for the end of the world (Mark 13:8; Rev. 6:5-8).

Third, there was a famine during the time, although it was limited to Palestine and Syria because of crop failures there and unusually heavy flooding in Egypt, a major grain-supplier. The writer of Acts, however, regards the hard times in the region as fulfillment of Agabus' words (Acts 19:28).

Fourth, Agabus did not claim that the Spirit told him to request money for Jerusalem. That was the voluntary decision of the Antiochene Christians. It should not be taken for granted. On the one hand, this church did not practice sharing wealth as had the Jerusalem church (see p. 31), nor was it as concerned to observe Torah scrupulously. Still, in time of need, the differences between Christianity in Jerusalem and in Antioch did not prevent a charitable act of solidarity—even on the part of gentile Christians. Nor did they say, "It serves them right; if they had kept their property they would have resources to buy the expensive grain now." Nor did they reason, "Let's collect some money for ourselves because if this is going to be a world-wide situation we're going to need it right here at home."

On the other hand, the Antiochene church had become more and more gentile, and it existed amid rising anti-Jewish feeling and outright hostility produced by the war in A.D. 66-70. Yet the memory of this act of compassion survived all that until the writer of Acts learned of it later. A church that keeps such a memory alive knows that its solidarity with Jerusalem Christians transcends war and prejudice.

Acts 13:1-3 reports the innovation suggested by five prophets and teachers. Barnabas and Saul/Paul we already know. The others are mentioned only here. Symeon was also known as Niger, the Latin for "black." Lucius was from north Africa. "Manaen" represents the Greek form of the Jewish name Menahem; that he was a member of Herod Antipas' court but living in Antioch suggests that he either belong to the upper class or worked for the royal household. Except perhaps for Symeon, none was a native of Antioch.

During the time of fasting—often regarded as preparation for receiving a revelation—they were inspired to have the church sponsor an outright mission to gentiles. It was one thing to evangelize one's gentile neighbors and associates; it was another to undertake a deliberate missionary effort to them. It is no coincidence that this development came from a cosmopolitan "interracial" church in a city having contacts with the whole region.

According to Acts, this was "the first missionary journey" of Paul (Acts 13—14). For the writer of Acts, the hostility of the Asia Minor Jews, in contrast with the favorable response of gentiles, means that now Christianity would become gentile, and that Israel forfeited its claim to be the true Israel (Acts 13:46-47; actually Paul never ceased trying to win Jews to the faith even though he regarded himself as the specially-chosen apostle to the gentiles).

At the end of the story of this journey, Acts reports that God had now, decisively and in a new way, "opened a door of faith to the gentiles" (Acts 14:27). That is what produced a major crisis for the church.

The Crisis and the Council

The crisis, as we noted at the beginning of this chapter, concerned the status of gentile believers. We do not know why the issue was not raised before. According to Acts some men from Judea arrived in Antioch and insisted, ". . . Unless you are circumcised according to the custom of Moses, you cannot be saved" (Acts 15:1). This means that a gentile who believes in Jesus but remains outside the chosen people is not saved at all.

One can imagine the furor this caused in Antioch. The issue was decided elsewhere, however—in Jerusalem where the Christian leadership convened (about A.D. 48) for what has come to be known as "the Jerusalem Council." Unfortunately, it is very difficult to get an accurate picture of what went on, for Acts 15 and Galatians 2 disagree at almost every point except the main one—that circumcision would not be required of gentiles. Had the decision gone the other way, it is doubtful whether Christianity would have survived the disastrous revolts of A.D. 66-70 and 132-135.

It is difficult for us to appreciate the conflict which was generated by the demand of the Judean brothers. Today, circumcision is an operation done fairly routinely to gentile baby boys, for whose parents it carries no religious meaning at all. Then, however, circumcision was regarded by Jews as a symbol of one's identification with the Jewish people. Male converts to Judaism were regularly circumcised, though a few exceptions are known. Moreover, "circumcision" gathered up a number of matters and conflicts, just as the word "amnesty" galvanized and focused all sorts of attitudes after the end of the American involvement in Vietnam.

We will note briefly some theological, social, and political aspects of "circumcision" as they may have been seen through the eyes of those who insisted upon it for gentile Christians.

• There were two theological claims. First, if Jesus is the expected Messiah of the Jewish people, must not the Messiah's people be Jews? Can one believe that Jesus is the Messiah and not accept the Torah, which calls for circumcision? Jesus never told anyone to disregard the Torah, and he himself was circumcised. Are these gentiles superior to the Torah and better than he? In short, one cannot be part of the *true* Israel (see chap. 2) and at the same time remain outside the actual Israel. To enter it gentile males must be circumcised. We might catch the force of this argument if we translate it into modern terms: You can't be a Christian and refuse to identify yourself with the church, can you? And the way to do that is to be baptized.

Second, Jewish hope included the conviction that gentiles would benefit from salvation in the New Age. But while the End of the old Age is near, it is not yet here. Only in the New Age would gentiles participate as gentiles. Meanwhile, gentiles who wish to be saved then must become Jews now.

• The social aspect of the conflict concerns the relation of Jewish and gentile Christians to one another. When Christians met in homes, they shared a common meal, part of which was the Lord's Supper. The separation of the Lord's Supper from the church supper came later, and for quite different reasons (see chap. 4). If gentile believers were uncircumcised, it would be awkward for many Jewish Christians to associate with them freely (see p. 43). Are we Jewish believers to be "defiled" every time we eat the Lord's Supper? Does this not alienate us from our kinfolk who are not Christians? Besides, who knows what gentiles will put on the table for supper?

• The political aspect has to do with the ties of the Jewish community in Antioch with Jews in Palestine. This crisis arose in the years of rising Jewish consciousness in Palestine. The more that Jews there felt it necessary to "circle the wagons" in order

59

to survive against the Procurators, the less tolerant they were of non-Palestinian Jews who abandoned Jewish customs. Palestinian Jewish Christians, in turn, would have been careful not to give the impression that believing in Jesus made them traitors to their own people.

Interestingly, a few years later Paul says that those who require gentiles to be circumcised do so in order that they themselves will not be persecuted (Gal. 6:12). This is a clear hint that Judean Christians asked their gentile brothers to be circumcised so as to take the pressure off themselves. The same strategy may have played a role earlier in Antioch. When we take these considerations together, and bear in mind the long-standing prejudice against gentiles and vice versa, we see that the church had to deal with a complicated and explosive issue.

Although Galatians 2:1-10 was written by one who was there, it is not a complete report. Paul is interested only in showing that he did not compromise his gospel, that it was recognized as fully valid, and that he had agreed only to gather money for the poor—which he was eager to do anyway. But he mentions some fascinating details. Paul's freedom to continue preaching (and founding churches) was confirmed—gentiles need not be circumcised.

Perhaps the presence of Titus helped win the day. Titus was an uncircumcised gentile convert who became Paul's associate (but who is never mentioned in the entire book af Acts). Paul apparently took Titus along because he wanted the Jerusalem Christians to see "a real live gentile Christian" and be forced to associate with him. Paul's tactic worked: Titus left Jerusalem as uncircumcised as he had arrived.

But Paul thinks the meeting was rigged. He speaks of "false brethren secretly brought in" to see for themselves just what Paul was up to. Unfortunately we do not know who they were. Although Paul implies that the leadership "waffled" instead of supporting his position forthrightly (he says they are "reputed to be pillars"), he insists that they did agree that his mission among the gentiles was as legitimate as was Peter's among the Jews, and that henceforth the one would concentrate on gentiles, the other on Jews.

The fact that gentiles were not required to be circumcised did not prevent them from accepting it if they wanted to, and it certainly did not mean that Jews should stop circumcising their sons. Circumcision was no longer a matter of principle, but only a custom. As Paul said later, "neither is circumcision anything nor uncircumcision" (Gal. 5:16). And if circumcision is a custom, then Christians can work out social situations as local conditions required.

One can see why Paul was infuriated later when travelling preachers appeared in the Galatian churches to insist that gentile believers must indeed be circumcised, that Paul was not a bona fide apostle, and that he had compromised himself in Jerusalem. We will explore his spirited response in chapter 5.

Perhaps Paul should have been forewarned by what happened later in Antioch (Gal. 2:11-13). Apparently everything was working out nicely until there arrived again some believers from Jerusalem, claiming the authority of James. They insisted that the agreement in Jerusalem really meant there must be separate groups of Christians: one for Jews who observed kosher, another for everyone else. So persuasive were they that even Barnabas and Peter stopped having meals (including the Lord's Supper) with gentile Christians.

What irritated Paul most was that these men did not act out of conviction but out of fear. Was it fear lest association with gentiles in Antioch threatened the safety of Jerusalem Christians? At any rate, Paul confronted Peter in public. Since Paul does not report what Peter said in return, we have no way of knowing who "won." So far as we know, Peter stayed and Paul left. As for his standing in Jerusalem, Romans 15:30-31 shows that when he was at the point of leaving for Jerusalem with the promised offering for the poor, he was not even sure it would be accepted. Nevertheless, there was no retreat from the decision itself: gentiles could be Christians and remain gentiles.

Acts 15:1-35 gives a quite different picture—so much so that it has been suggested that it reports a different meeting! In Acts, it is Peter who supplies the argument, Paul who provides the case histories, and James who proposes the solution. In Acts 15:7-11 Peter refers back to the story of the conversion of Cornelius (emphasized before by repeating aspects of it three times in Acts 10:1—11:8).

Peter argues that gentiles must not be burdened with the law which Jews had never been able to keep anyway, and that the salvation of Jews and gentiles rests on precisely the same foundation—the grace of Christ. Besides, since gentiles too received the Holy Spirit, this gift does not depend on circumcision. Paul merely reports his experiences among gentiles in order to back up Peter's argument. James ignores what Paul had to say and proposes a compromise in view of Peter's argument. Circumcision will not be required, but gentiles must observe a minimum of what the Torah requires: no idolatry, no sexual license, no eating of meat improperly slaughtered. These regulations were not invented on the spot, but were the traditional minimum requirements for gentiles living among Jews (Lev. 17).

One problem with this account is that Paul insists that the only requirement was the collection for the poor, but this is not mentioned by Acts at all. Another is that Paul never mentions the letter which Acts says he actually carried back with him, and even Acts has James tell Paul about such a letter years later in Jerusalem (Acts 21:25). The regulations clearly deal with the basis on which Jewish and gentile Christians may associate with one another. This solved a problem which arose *later* in Antioch, as Paul himself shows. Probably these requirements were adopted after Paul confronted Peter and then left the city.

The house churches must have constituted a rather remarkable church in Antioch. All these developments occurred within a span of about fifteen years. Repeatedly this church crossed frontiers. It was the first "interracial" church. It was the first to engage in Christian relief work. From it came the first deliberate effort to take the gospel to gentiles. Its representative, Paul, was the first powerful Christian theologian, and the first to argue that gentiles could be Christians without becoming practicing Jews and that Jews could continue to be Jews—a view which made worldwide, ecumenical, pluralistic Christianity possible. It was at Antioch that the believers in Jesus achieved sufficient distinctiveness to be known as "Christ's people"—Christians.

If the regulations of Acts 15:20 were first adopted at Antioch, this church also had political savvy. It required its gentile members to obey the law by making them observe what they were doing already. This allowed its Jewish members to continue to live among Jews in peace. A pretty good record for the first generation—or any, for that matter.

DIVERGING TRENDS IN THE SECOND GENERATION

For knowledge of the second generation we depend almost entirely on what we can infer from texts which may have been written at Antioch. In the previous chapter, (see pp. 36-38) we saw how and why texts which tell about Jesus can be used to show us certain things about the Christians. Here we shall see what the Gospels of Matthew and John can disclose about Antiochene Christianity in the A.D. 90's.

The Gospel and the Gospels

At the beginning, the word "gospel" (good news) referred to the spoken message about the meaning of Jesus for human salvation. Mark was the first (around A.D. 70) to use the word for a written account of Jesus' ministry. Until then the words and stories about Jesus circulated by word of mouth, either as individual items or in short collections. This oral tradition continued alongside the written gospels for many years.

One important collection of Jesus' words was made before Mark. We do not know who compiled it, nor where this was done (probably in Palestine or Syria, perhaps even in Antioch). The compilation no longer exists, but much of it can be reconstructed from Matthew and Luke who used it. Scholars call this Q. The authors of Matthew and Luke used Mark and Q, as well as other stories and sayings which each of them knew.

How Matthew and Luke used these materials (they almost always make some changes either in wording or sequence) reveals the emphases of these later Gospels. These emphases, in turn, can tell us what was going on in the churches for which they were written.

It is more difficult to use the Gospel of John in this way. In the case of Matthew and Luke we can see how each of them used Mark, but since John did not use any Gospel we now have it is more difficult to detect just what he used or how he did so. It is clear, however, that John too is the end-result of a long process in which older traditions are combined with comments and with other material.

John 3 shows how theological reflection follows older material like a commentary. The RSV ends Jesus' words to Nicodemus at 3:15, as the quotation marks show. This means that John 3:16-21 is the Evangelist's comment, rather than part of what Jesus himself said. An example of material which was added is chapter 21. John 20:30-31 clearly ended the Gospel at an earlier stage. Likewise, chapters 15—17 were added to the story of the Last Supper, because one can go from 14:31 to 18:1 and discover that the story moves ahead smoothly. Although it is more difficult to get a sharp profile of John's congregations than it is of those which used Matthew, some important things can be seen, and they are enough for us here.

Both Matthew and John were written in the 90's. Scholars have long believed that Matthew was probably written in Antioch or near by. In learning about Matthew's church, we therefore learn about Antioch. On the other hand, John has been associated with

Ephesus. However, there are reasons to think that John was written in Antioch instead.

John's church is at odds with the synagogue which has expelled Christians (John 9:22; 16:2), an action resulting from changes in the liturgy (see p. 29). This reflects the influence of the Palestinian rabbinate on other Jewish communities and is more likely to have been the case in Antioch than in far-off Ephesus. Moreover, this is the same situation to which Matthew responds (Matt. 10:16-23).

The language and thought-world of John is similar to that of a collection of early Christian hymns called "The Odes of Solomon," written in Antioch or Syria but not Ephesus. Ephesus was a major center for Paul and his followers, and his letters may have been collected there; but there is no trace of Paul's influence in John.

Only Matthew 16:13-20 and John 21 emphasize Peter's responsibility for the church, and reflect his role in the church which told these stories. That points to Antioch, not Ephesus. In other words, although no one can prove that John was written at Antioch (or at Ephesus!), we have a high enough degree of probability to proceed on this basis.

By considering briefly some technical aspects of Gospel study, we see why one can learn about Christians in Antioch from Matthew and John. Two consequences emerge.

First, Matthew and John are quite different; one has only to read them through one after the other to see this on every page. If they were written in the same city (or area) in the same decade, then they must have been written for quite different congregations. (In the first century, each Christian community had but one written Gospel. It would be some time before churches had four Gospels side by side.) In other words, Matthew and John show us different Christian communities within Antiochene Christianity. In a large city this need not surprise us, especially since the greater the number of house churches the greater the opportunity for different styles of Christianity to emerge.

Second, since both Matthew and John are the end-products of using texts and traditions, the types of Christianity represented by them must have existed side by side for some years. Naturally, they shared many things as well. We will note briefly some similarities and differences.

Different Responses to Basic Questions

How is Christianity related to Judaism? As we saw, after A.D. 70 the Pharisaism Jesus knew became rabbinic Judaism. Part of the rabbis' program was to consolidate their influence over other Jewish communities. This involved squeezing out the Christians. When Matthew and John wrote of Jesus' conflicts with the Pharisees, therefore, they were not simply recording the tradition of what he said and did; they were telling the story to help their own congregations deal with the synagogues they knew. They blended the tradition with their own experience. They were trying to let the words and deeds of Jesus speak to their own times. Whenever someone today says, "Jesus taught that love was the most important thing," exactly the same sort of thing is taking place. The tradition is being made to speak in today's language.

The new situation forced John and Matthew to think through again the relation of Christianity to Judaism. Is Christianity the fulfillment of Judaism, or is it an alternative to it? Does Christianity represent the real point of Judaism which the synagogue was distorting, or is the difference between them much deeper? Matthew answered Yes to the first part of these questions, John affirmed the second half.

No one in the New Testament insists more than Matthew that Jesus came as the fulfillment of the Old Testament. Right from the start, the marvellous things that occurred when Jesus was conceived and born are said to bring to pass certain lines in the Scriptures (e.g., Matt. 1:22-23; 2:13-15). In the Sermon on the Mount Jesus provides the proper interpretation of the Torah (especially Matt. 5:21-48), and of the three basic forms of piety —alms, prayer, and fasting (Matt. 6:1-18). Thus Matthew shows that Jesus did not come to do away with the Scripture but to fulfill it, and has him say so, too (Matt. 5:17-19).

Among other reasons, Matthew may have been responding to the accusation of the rabbis: "You Christians abandon the Torah." "Not so," says Matthew; "we are closer to doing what it really means than you." (Matthew 15:12-14 has Jesus accuse the Pharisees of being blind guides of the blind. His basic charge against them is hypocrisy. In chapter 23 he compiled sayings of Jesus into a seven-fold denunciation, "Woe to you, scribes, Pharisees, hypocrites!" The common meaning of "Pharisee" = "hypocrite" comes from Matthew's polemic.) Unfortunately, "they preach but do not practice" (Matt. 23:3).

For Matthew, the righteousness required by God has been stated in the Torah and has been rightly interpreted by Jesus' word and deed. One who follows Jesus does not become a hypocrite but a God-like person (Matt. 5:48).

65

Matthew thinks that Judaism has not only missed the meaning of Torah, but that in rejecting Jesus it has forfeited its claim to be the people of God. This is clearly the way he understands the parable in Matthew 21:33-44. He regards the fall of Jerusalem as God's punishment. Jesus had restricted his mission and that of his followers to the Jews (Matt. 10:5-6), but that only made the rejection more tragic. Now, after his resurrection, the Messiah's people are to be found among all nations (Matt. 28:16-20). In other words, Matthew is both very Jewish in his outlook and against Judaism at the same time.

John is more hostile to Judaism than is Matthew. For one thing, whereas Matthew aims his polemic against the religious leaders, John repeatedly lumps everyone together as "the Jews." John agrees with Matthew, of course, that Jesus fulfills the Old Testament (e.g., John 1:43-45; 5:39; 12:14-15). Yet he also has Jesus make a blanket indictment: "none of you keeps the law" (John 7:19), and speak of "your law" as if Jesus himself were not a Jew (John 8:17; 10:34). Of course he knows Jesus was a Jew, but John sees a deep hostility between Jesus and "the Jews" because they usually stand for the world which is in darkness (John 1:9-11). Indeed, they are "of the devil" even though they think their father is God (John 8:42-44).

In the Gospel of John, Jesus does not provide the true interpretation of the Torah because for John Christianity is not the truth of the Torah which Judaism missed. Actually, the Torah is a pointer to Jesus. Jesus does not fulfill Judaism but transforms it, as the stories of turning water to wine and the cleansing of the temple make clear symbolically (John 2:1-22). In fact, Judaism as a system of salvation is now as irrelevant as the Samaritan temple because what God seeks is spiritual worship (John 4:20-24).

For John, the Christian does not strive for a righteousness which exceeds that of Judaism, as Matthew put it (Matt. 5:21). Rather one is to obey a new commandment altogether (John 13:34-35). Repeatedly Jesus speaks of *my* commandment as the thing that matters now (John 14:15, 21; 15:10, 12-17). Never is it Jesus' aim to make clear how one is to keep Moses' commandment properly; that no longer matters. John's Jesus would never have answered the question, "What good deed must I do to inherit eternal life?" by "Keep the commandments," as Matthew's Jesus did (Matt. 19:16-22). In John the way to eternal life is the new birth.

For John, Jesus does not teach the way to salvation, he *is* the way; he does not bring the light but *is* the light; he does not explain the truth but *is* the truth, and no one comes to God except through him (John 14:6). One might put the difference this way: in Matthew, Jesus takes one to the right understanding of the Torah and thereby shows that he is the Messiah; in John, a right understanding of the Torah takes one to Jesus, the only revelation of God (John 1:18).

We have devoted so much attention to Matthew's and John's attitude toward Judaism because today Christianity must free itself from the evil consequences of taking them at face value. We can understand why Matthew and John wrote the way they did, but we need not accept their views as our own. Indeed, the more we understand how their attitudes were shaped by the historical circumstances of the day, the clearer it is that our circumstances are wholly different and so call for a different answer to the same question.

Today it is not the Christians who are harassed by the synagogue. Rather, it is the Jews who have been persecuted for centuries by the Christians. Today we know that Pharisees were not simply hypocrites (and certainly not the only ones). We know also that in John Jesus attacks Judaism as he does because this is part of John's theological view of how the Light attacks human darkness, and that John does not give us what Jesus actually said. Since in John "the Jews" stand for the world in darkness and hostility to God, one must ask this question: If John were writing about what happens when the Light comes into darkness today, what would be today's equivalent of "the Jews?"

What sort of community is the church to be? This question is as important in the last quarter of the twentieth century as it was in the last quarter of the first. Indeed, every generation asks it afresh and struggles toward an acceptable range of answers. A decade ago, Christians in America were polarized over the church's involvement in social change, some insisting on more participation, others contending that its top priority must remain changing persons (evangelism), who then might change society. There was no way that this issue could have arisen in the first century because the whole idea that ordinary people could change society was as unknown as a trip to the moon. What the church then had to think through was how to be faithful to the gospel under those circumstances, especially the growing alienation from Judaism.

Matthew accused the rabbis of losing sight of what is really important, of "straining out a gnat and swallowing a camel," of neglecting what really matters according to the law itself—justice (righteousness), mercy, and faith (Matt. 23:23-24). Matthew used the words and deeds of Jesus to show what these actually mean. The church, as the community of the Messiah, needs to know what it will be held accountable for on Judgment Day.

67

According to Matthew 7:21-23, it will not be enough to believe in Jesus, to speak prophetically and do good in his name; what will matter on Judgment Day is whether one has done God's will (which includes believing in Jesus, of course). Only if the Christian confession of Jesus as Lord is matched with appropriate deeds will one's righteousness exceed that of the scribes and Pharisees (Matt. 6:20). To enter the kingdom one must have God-like integrity (which is what "perfect" means in Matt. 5:48). Matthew even insists that one must not keep score on good deeds done but leave it to God to give the reward (Matt. 6:2-4). Nowhere is this made more clear than in the parable of the Judgment, where those who showed mercy did not realize that they had done so to the Christ who had identified with the needy (Matt. 25:31-46).

Why did Matthew emphasize doing God's will? Why did he put together the sayings of Jesus to make the point so powerfully? Not simply to make sure they were not forgotten! There were people in his church who "talked a good game" but had no integrity. They, he thinks, are wolves in sheep's clothing (Matt. 7:15-20), and the church must be warned against these "false prophets."

Matthew is confronting Christians who think that a commitment to Jesus is enough. Some may actually argue that being a Christian excuses one from doing the law (Matt. 5:19). They think that their salvation is guaranteed by their confession, baptism, and reception of the Spirit. They equate being in the church with being in the Kingdom of God. Not so, says Matthew. The church is the community in which one prepares properly to enter the Kingdom when the Son of Man comes. On Judgment Day there will be surprises for everyone.

But Matthew also had to contend with an opposite tendency—some insisted that the church must be so much like the Kingdom that anyone who does not meet the requirements is to be expelled. They insist on a "pure" church. To deal with them, he includes the parables in Matthew 13:24-30 (explained in vv. 36-43) and 13:47-50. These parables insist that until the End, the church will include all sorts of people, that only God has the right to identify the saved, and that he will do so at the End, not before.

The warning against handing out verdicts on fellow-Christians in Matthew 7:1-5 responds to this same problem. Matthew would hardly have insisted on this point if he did not have to deal with Christians who were eager to judge one another. These teachings of Jesus are, in fact, found only in Matthew.

Does Matthew imply that the church should be indifferent about the Christians who fail to measure up? By no means. Much of chapter 18 is devoted to various aspects of church discipline. The first discipline, he implies, is self-imposed (Matt. 18:7-9). Then, before dealing with the disciplining of others, he writes the parable of the stray sheep in order to point out that God is concerned for the erring Christian (18:10-14). Next, he spells out actual procedures for dealing with the straying Christian. Those who reject the duly administered process of admonishing are to be shunned—an utterly serious act for someone in a house church (18:15-20).

The possibilities for restoration and forgiveness have no limit (18:21-22) because those who have been forgiven so much by God must not limit the forgiving they will do among one another (18:23-35). (This chapter shows clearly how the placement of the material has been planned carefully by the Evangelist.) Since the Judgment may come at any time, it is dangerous to be alienated from a brother or sister; in fact, one should not even go to church unreconciled (Matt. 5:21-26). Moreover, Christians should pray for those who persecute them (Matt. 5:43-47).

Matthew is trying to guide the church into a middle way between a lax attitude toward the requirements of righteousness on the one hand, and an over-eager concern on the part of some that only "real" Christians be allowed in the church, and who take it upon themselves to determine who they may be. There must be discipline, but it is to be orderly, and always carried out in the context of limitless mercy and forgiveness.

Once we see how sensitive Matthew is to such practical questions, we are amazed at the way John deals with them—that is, hardly deals with them at all. In John 1—12 we have an exposition, from various angles, of what happens when the Light, the incarnate Son of God, encounters darkness. In chapters 13—17 (the farewell discourses) Jesus is alone with his disciples. It is here that we catch most glimpses of John's church. What we can see, however, must be inferred from certain theological emphases and the language used to express them; the church appears only indirectly.

To begin with, as John understands it, the church repeats the situation of Jesus in the world. Just as the world hated him, so it hates the church. The reason is that neither Jesus nor the church are "of" the world (John 17:14, 16) but rather are "of" God (John 1:13). To be "of" something is to derive one's life and values from it, to depend on it and to obey its will. It is in this light that we must understand the accusation, "You are of the devil" (John 8:44). Likewise, the new birth is necessary because without it one lives "of" the flesh, not "of" the Spirit (John 3:6). By believing in Jesus, the disciples, like him, are now "of" God not "of" the world, though they are very much in it. Indeed, being an alien in the world is a mark of salvation.

Which Christians understand themselves (and Jesus) in this way? This is manifestly the thinking of a group that experiences hostility, and which in turn understands that hostility as a sign of its salvation. In John's case, we see an intense feeling of rejection and persecution by the synagogue, as John 16:1-4 shows (as does 15:18-21). John's outlook is much more like that of the Anabaptists in the sixteenth century or the Jehovah's Witnesses in the twentieth than it is of mainline, establishment churches which regard themselves as pretty much at home in the world and responsible to it. Inevitably establishment Christianity emphasizes the "spirituality" of John because it no longer knows the experience of being an oppressed minority. But apparently that is what John's church was.

Not surprisingly, when John emphasizes love, he has in mind almost entirely the love of one believer for another and their common love for Christ. All the love commands emphasize this reciprocal love (John 13:34-35; 15:12-17). Not a word is ever said about loving one's fellow human (the neighbor). The First Epistle of John, which belongs to the same strand of Christianity, actually forbids loving the world and things in it (1 John 2:15-17), just as it commands that Christians love each other (1 John 3: 11-18; 4:7-21). The Christians are "of God" but the whole world is in the hands of the devil (1 John 5:19). Nor do the Johannine writings say a word about forgiving the persecutors. Rather, it is a closed circle: those who love Jesus love each other.

John's emphasis on mutual love among Christians also reflects the situation of harrassment. John 16:1 shows that there is danger of "falling away." In times of pressure, groups often begin to fragment, one pulling away in order to avoid embarrassment, another jockeying for influence in times of hesitation, another dividing the group by proposing compromises, and so on. In this light one can understand why the farewell discourses begin with the example of Jesus washing the disciples feet: the Christians are to serve one another as he served them (John 13:1-17).

Moreover, John warns his readers that they should not take their salvation for granted. In the allegory of the vine (John 15:1-11) Jesus warns that the branches exist only insofar as they are "in" the stock; whoever does not stand by his faith in Jesus is pruned away like a dry twig. But in contrast with Matthew, John

70

says not a word of how this actually takes place. There is no hint of disciplinary procedures, such as Matthew 18:15-20 provide, nor any statement which implies who is responsible for the pruning. Instead, the passive form of the verb implies that God himself will prune the dead wood.

Diversity and Unity in Antioch

Many other differences between Matthew and John could be noted. Accumulating such differences would, however, simply reinforce what we already know: John and Matthew were written within, and for quite different strands of Christianity, each with its own traditions. The differences are there even if these Gospels had been written a thousand miles apart. The likelihood that they were written in Antioch, however, means that Christianity there was diversified, not uniform. But what did those Christians have in common?

First of all, these types of Christianity were not isolated from one another, even if each developed in its own way. They shared certain traditions about Jesus, though the forms of the tradition differed; we think of the importance of John the Baptist or the story of Jesus' cleansing of the temple. Moreover, they shared the same Greek version of the Old Testament as well as the conviction that it must be read in light of the coming of Christ. Above all, they shared the essential point—that Jesus was God's way of bringing salvation, and that he had been resurrected. For all the differences, there is no doubt that each would have acknowledged the other as authentically Christian.

In the second place, both strands looked to Peter and not to James. In later traditions, Peter came to be regarded as Antioch's first bishop. He was followed by Evodius, who is said to have been bishop for 29 years; we know almost nothing else about him. It is reported, however, that his (lost) epistle told how Christ baptized Peter, who in turn baptized the other disciples. This tradition attempts to establish a continuous line of authority from Christ to the later bishops.

Matthew and John have other ways of tracing Peter's authority to Jesus. In the Gospel of John the resurrected Lord assigned Peter the role of pastor (shepherd) of the church (John 21:15-19). For some reason, in the Fourth Gospel Peter's responsibility is not connected with his being renamed Peter (=Cephas or Rock). John 1:40-42 reports that Jesus gave him this name the moment he became a disciple.

The best-known story of how Simon came to be called Rock and given responsibility for the church is in Matthew 16:13-20.

71

Here Matthew inserts vv. 17-19 into the story of Peter's confession which he found in Mark, and it is precisely these verses which explain the name and confer the authority. Today Catholic and Protestant scholars agree that "on this rock I will build my church" refers to Peter the Rock, not to his confession. In Matthew 18:18 the authority to "bind" and "loose" (=make decisions for the community) is shared with the whole church—as if to imply that Peter is "first among equals." John does not have this famous Caesarea-Philippi story, but does have Peter make a confession of faith in John 6:66-69.

Our concern here is to see what purpose these stories served and what that tells us about early Christianity. Such stories were told because they account for Peter's place in Antioch. On this point, the congregations for which John and Matthew wrote agreed. Looking to Peter for leadership was one of the things that united Antiochene Christianity and distinguished it from Jerusalem where James was in charge.

FRAGMENTATION AND CONSOLIDATION

We have portrayed second-generation Christianity in Antioch as expressed in two rather different Gospels, Matthew and John. Probably some house churches looked to Matthew while others relied on John. These groups existed within one church because they shared certain beliefs and practices, such as baptism and eucharist, and had a common tradition of Peter's leadership. But how long could this continue?

In the third generation, we see both fragmentation and consolidation. Some wanted to make Christianity more Jewish, while others were even more hostile to Judaism than John had been. The one who tried to unify the church by rejecting both extremes was the martyr-bishop, Ignatius, deeply influenced by both Matthew and John. In him we see a growing reliance on the institutional church and its sacraments.

For reasons not known, Ignatius had been tried and sentenced in Antioch, but was being sent to Rome as a prisoner, where he was killed by beasts around A.D. 110. Also unknown is the reason he was being taken by land through Asia Minor. In any case, while enroute he wrote letters to six churches and one bishop (Polycarp of Smyrna). Although none of them went to Antioch, they imply a good deal about what had been going on there.

Polarizing Developments

Many factors were at work, doubtless, in the polarization of Christians at Antioch. Perhaps the two opposite developments had at least some of their roots in the house churches in which Matthew and John were produced. At least one can see certain continuities. Ignatius opposes a tendency to regard Christianity as a version, the true one to be sure, of Judaism. Some continued to observe Sabbath as well as Sunday, and followed other Jewish customs as well, though apparently not circumcision—that had been settled. They seem to have regarded Jesus as a great teacher, probably as the greatest of a series going back to Moses and the prophets.

In any case, Ignatius objects to anything which blurs the difference between Christianity and Judaism, and which regards Judaism as its norm. He writes the Magnesians, "It is absurd to speak of Jesus Christ and to practice Judaism; for Christianity did not believe in Judaism, but Judaism in Christianity, in which all people believing in God are gathered" (10:3).[1] To the Philadelphians he wrote, "If anyone should interpret Judaism to you, do not listen to him; for it is better to hear Christianity from a Jew than to hear Judaism from a gentile" (6:1).

At issue was whether Christianity is something to be understood in light of the Old Testament and Judaism, or whether these are to be understood in light of Christianity and Jesus. Someone told him, "Unless I find it in the original documents, I do not believe in the gospel." When he replied, "It is written in the Scripture," they answered, "That is exactly the question." For Ignatius, he goes on, the "orignials" are Jesus Christ because the Old Testament, being anticipation and prediction, takes its meaning from Christ the fulfillment. Christ is "the Father's door, through which enter Abraham and Isaac and Jacob and the prophets and the apostles and the church" (Phild. 8—9).

Although Ignatius does not identify the groups holding such views in Antiochene congregations, we know that there were Jewish Christians who regarded Jesus as the great prophet but not as the incarnation of the Word of God. They hated Paul and viewed Hellenized Christianity as compromised with paganism. Also they circulated their own gospels (only fragments of which have survived as quotations). These Jewish Christian groups were found especially in Syria, and perhaps in Antioch as well. There they might have also tried to influence gentile Christians.

---

[1]From *Early Christian Fathers*, Vol. 1, Ed. Cyril C. Richardson, The Westminster Press, 1956, p. 97.

Much more of a danger, at least as Ignatius saw it, was the opposite development—an interpretation of Christianity which rejected Judaism and the fundamental theological motif inherited from it, the positive meaning of creation. This development emphasized the divinity of Christ, indeed over-emphasized it because it denied that he was really and fully human. He only *seemed* to be human; he was actually divinity disguised as a man.

This whole movement is known as Docetism (pronounced doe-setism, from the Greek word meaning "to seem"). It had many forms, appeared in all sorts of places and was taught by various theologians in the second century, among whom was Marcion. Docetism is closely linked with Gnosticism (from *gnosis,* the word for "knowledge"). Since Docetism has a particular view of Christ, it exists only in Christianity as a heresy. Gnosticism, on the other hand, is a way of salvation found both inside and outside of Christianity; one of its influences in Christianity was a docetic view of Christ.

In the gnostic point of view, flesh and matter are evil; they oppress the soul—a spark of the divine now imprisoned in the body. Salvation comes when the soul receives knowledge *(gnosis)* of what it really is, where it came from, and where it can go after the body dies; then the soul is released to escape the world altogether. Exactly when this thinking began to influence Christianity is debated, but it seems likely that the process began already in Paul's time.

In any case, in the second century we find gnostic Christian groups, many of who found John's gospel congenial to their thinking. Indeed, the earliest commentary on John we know of was written by a gnostic, Heracleon, near the end of the second century. What gnostics liked about John was the point that the Savior is not of this world but descended to it and returned, as well as John's insistence that Christians to are not of this world. At the end of the second century, Bishop Irenaeus in Gaul (now France) showed in detail that the gnostics were twisting John's meaning. From the start, Christians with docetic views of Christ presented a challenge to the church.

Unfortunately, Ignatius did not name his opponents. We do know, however, that one of the gnostic teachers in Antioch at the time was Saturninus. According to Irenaeus, he taught that the God of the Jews was one of the evil angels who created the world and the human body. He also taught that the real God sent a spark of life into Adam's body, and that after death this spark could return to its source. Christ came down from this real God to destroy the God of the Jews. Christ only seemed to be human;

had he been born or been a real man, he would not have been the Savior but part of the problem. An especially evil angel is Satan, who opposes the God of the Jews and is the origin of sex and marriage. Saturninus' disciples, therefore, rejected sex.

They evidently regarded Jesus as the savior from creation and its Creator, from Satan, and from the Old Testament. What Saturninus represented was the opposite of the "Judaisers" in Antioch. It is also clear that he could have found passages in John which supported his views, given a little ingenuity in interpretation.

Ignatius counters by repeatedly insisting on the reality of the incarnation, especially the reality of Christ's sufferings and resurrection. "He is truly of the family of David according to the flesh [a paraphrase of Rom. 1:3], Son of God according to the will and power of God, truly born of a virgin, baptized by John in order that all righteousness might be fulfilled by him [this explanation is found only in Matt. 3:15]. In the time of Pontius Pilate and Herod the Tetrarch he was truly nailed in the flesh for our sakes [nails are mentioned only in John 20:25]." With a certain bitterness he says that if the Lord only seemed to do these things, then he only seemed to be a prisoner! (Symr. 1;4).

Ignatius is not the only one of the time to oppose Docetism. The First Letter of John, probably written after the Gospel of John and by someone else in John's congregations, opposes docetic Christians throughout. How can one know whether what a Christian teacher claims to come from the Spirit of God was true or false? First John 4:2-3 lays down a rule: "Every spirit which confesses that Jesus Christ has come in the flesh is of God, and every spirit which does not confess Jesus is not of God." This is the clearest anti-docetic statement in the whole New Testament. Moreover, the text goes on to say that whoever denies the reality of the incarnation manifests the spirit of the anti-Christ. Apparently, the church had split over the issue, because according to 1 John 2:18-19 there are many "anti-Christs" and they have already left the church.

Ignatius said that they were staying away from the Lord's Supper because "they do not confess the eucharist to be the flesh of our savior Jesus Christ which suffered for the sake of our sins, which the Father raised in his goodness" (Smyr. 7). Under the circumstances, he says it is proper to stay away from such people altogether, both in public and in private. Perhaps he gave this advice to the church before he left Antioch. In any case, those with docetic ideas are beginning to form their own groups, doubtless under the leadership of persons like Saturninus. Christianity, which had begun as a sect within Judaism, now is confronted by its own splinter groups which claim to have the real truth of the matter.

It is difficult to know who belonged to such groups. It appears, however, that they were a somewhat elitist group of gentile Christians who looked down on ordinary Christians. Ignatius also accuses them of lacking Christian charity: "They have no concern for love, nor for widows, nor for orphans, nor for the oppressed, nor for the prisoner, nor for him released from prison, nor for the hungry and thirsty" (Smyr. 6). Why should they have been concerned for the physical circumstances of people, if the flesh and all that goes with it is evil, and if salvation is a matter of having proper knowledge about the soul and its destiny? Ignatius was not the last, unfortunately, to confront groups who were so concerned for spiritual things that they neglected love or concern for the physical hurts of people.

Consolidating the Church

It would be a long time before Docetism and Gnosticism were overcome. This was because many persons and churches were attracted to these doctrines, and because the church developed its strategy as it went along. It has been said that the church came to rely on the canon, the creed, and the clergy. In Ignatius' time, these were not yet developed. The canon itself still had to be defined. As we saw in chapter 1, it was Marcion who forced the church to do this, perhaps sooner than would have occurred otherwise. At the turn of the century, our four Gospels were not the only ones being read and Christians of all stripes could still appeal to unwritten traditions about Jesus.

The creed, especially the "Apostles Creed," was developed later, probably in Rome (Ignatius never appears to quote a creed). In any case, whoever believes "in God the Father Almighty, maker of heaven and earth" rejects the basis of Docetism and Gnosticism. To confess that Christ "was born of the Virgin Mary, suffered under Pontius Pilate, was crucified, dead, and buried" was to insist on what Docetists denied. By making the creed the norm of Christian faith, the church made other views heretical. The clergy also had to consolidate, and Ignatius is an important figure in the process.

Ignatius was concerned for the whole, universal church; he is the first to speak of "the catholic church." More important, he emphasizes the role of the clergy, which in his time consisted of bishops, elders (presbyters), and deacons. Yet he does not view them as rigidly stratified as in an army. He is confident that if the churches will stand by their duly constituted clergy, they will adhere to the truth, for the clergy represent the authentic chain of tradition.

> Let all of you follow the bishop, as Jesus Christ follows the Father, and follow the presbytery as if it were the apostles; respect the deacons as the command of God. Let no one do any of the things that have to do with the church without the bishop. Let that be regarded as a valid eucharist which is overseen by the bishop or by one he appoints. When the bishop appears, there let the congregation be, just as wherever Jesus Christ is, there the catholic church is. It is not lawful either to baptize or have a love feast without the bishop, but whatever he approves, this is also well-pleasing to God, so that whatever you do may be sure and valid.

—Letter to the Smyrneans. Chatper 8.

Ignatius believed, probably correctly, that since the clergy were the guardians of the tradition, whoever challenged their interpretation of Christianity was challenging their authority. Theological struggles were at the same time power struggles. The clearest sign of this in the New Testament in 3 John: "I have written something to the church, but Diotrephes, who likes to put himself first, does not acknowledge my authority. . . . He refuses to welcome the brethren, and also stops those who want to welcome them and puts them out of the church." If only we knew what lay behind these lines! And wouldn't it be interesting to hear Diotrephes' side of the story?

Had there not developed strong leadership in the churches, Christianity might have become so gnosticised that it would not have survived. On the other hand, the possibility that the clergy, including bishops, could embody a distorted Christianity never occurred to Ignatius. He could not foresee that a century and a half later, the bishop of Antioch would be the heretic, Paul (from Samosata in eastern Syria), who lived like a prince and was followed by a retinue of women, or that it would take a council of about eighty bishops to get rid of him.

Fortunately for Ignatius, he got word that the church in Antioch had composed its differences. He asked the Philadelphians to send an emissary to Antioch to join with others to celebrate the new harmony. He may never have learned that it was probably only a truce. In Rome, his desire to die a martyr was fulfilled.

Chapter Four
CRISES OF CHRISTIAN FREEDOM

Can one claim too much freedom in the name of the gospel? If someone asserts that the Spirit has made him or her radically free from customs and ordinary morality, can one criticize this asserted freedom without criticizing the Spirit? How does one know whether what is claimed to be the work of the Spirit really is from the Spirit? What is really going on when one advertises his or her gifts of the Spirit? How does spirituality affect sexuality? These questions were being asked in Corinth nineteen centuries ago. No church in the New Testament is more fascinating than this one—nor more contemporary.

So much of Paul's letter-writing was directed to the Corinthians because they gave him the most trouble. In fact, were it not for problems in his churches, which he could not deal with directly, he would not have written letters—certainly not the ones we have. Each of them was occasioned by a difficulty. Curiously, Acts never mentions any problems in his churches. In the next chapter we shall see the reason for this. Right now we shall first see Paul's work in Greece as a whole, then trace his relationship to Corinth. That will give us perspective for seeing the crises of Christian freedom there.

THE APOSTLE TO THE GENTILES

The new churches around the Aegean Sea emerged in response to Paul's preaching after he left Antioch, where he had opposed Peter (see p. 61). According to Acts 16:6-10 Paul took the gospel from Asia Minor to Europe as a result of a vision. He began in Macedonia (now northeastern Greece) and worked his way southward to Corinth, where he stayed about two years. We know he was in Corinth in A.D. 50-51 because Acts 18:12 mentions the Roman Proconsul, Gallio, whose term of office we know. The story of Paul's work in Greece is told in Acts 16:12—18:17.

78

He began at Philippi, where the first converts were a woman merchant and her household. Acts, however, tells us nothing about this church, but is interested only in the dramatic stories of Paul's imprisonment. Yet this was the only church from which he later accepted financial support (Phil. 4:10-20). From Philippi he went to Thessalonika (now Salonika), where the new congregation included Jews as well as Gentiles. Again he was the occasion for civil disturbance, and left the city after dark. Although at Beroea his preaching in the synagogue had a better response, again he was forced to leave, this time going to Athens. Paul's preaching there was hardly a success, though Acts uses the occasion to show how he preached to the intellectuals of the day (Acts 17:16-34).

Most of these new Christians were not Jews; probably many were Gentiles who had been attending the synagogues as "God-fearers" (Acts 17:4-17; 18:7). They were not as poor as is sometimes said on the basis of 1 Corinthians 1:26. Probably, these congregations included craftsmen and workers, and lower middle class families together with their slaves. Although 2 Corinthians 8:2 speaks of the poverty of the Macedonians, the Philippians could afford to support Paul. Moreover, some of the Corinthians evidently had enough wealth that they could be sued in court (1 Cor. 6:1-6). It would be some time before the upper classes or government officials were part of these congregations. Clearly, women played an important role in these new churches, as we shall see later.

The Gospel in a Boom Town

The Corinth Paul knew was a thriving new city which had been rebuilt recently. The Romans had destroyed the old city in 146 B.C. For a century it was abandoned until Julius Caesar ordered it rebuilt as a Roman colony. The colonists were freedmen (former slaves) from Italy, but the population was soon cosmopolitan, and included a Jewish community.

Corinth prospered because of its location—near the narrow isthmus which connects Greece's largest peninsula (the Peloponnese) with the mainland. Ships were unloaded on one side and their cargoes dragged on rollers across the three and one-half miles of land to the other side where theye were reloaded. When Nero visited the city in A.D. 66 or 67 he planned to dig a canal here, but the project was not completed until the nineteenth century. Today the canal is in use, but Corinth is only a small village beside the once busy and increasingly beautiful boom town.

Corinth prospered also because of its religious shrines. The sanctuary of Asclepius, the god of healing, was at the spring. South of the city stands a huge rock bluff, the Acro-Corinth (over 1800 feet high), on top of which stood the temple of Aphrodite, goddess of love and prosperity. In Paul's time, however, this shrine had lost its former importance. The major temple in Corinth was dedicated to Apollo, and its remains still form the landmark.

Worshippers donated wealth to these shrines out of gratitude to the gods. The shrines also brought commerce to the area, the way religious conventions bring business to our own cities. Moreover, since Corinth was the provincial capital, there was always a certain amount of government business. Corinth was also a sports center, for the Isthmian Games were held there periodically. Athens may have symbolized the intellectual culture of Greece, but in Paul's time the action was in Corinth.

When Paul arrived (Acts 18:1-3), he went to the Jewish quarter where he found some refugees from Rome and made friends with Aquila and his wife Prisca (called Priscilla in Acts). Evidently they were Christians. Since they, like Paul, were in the tent business, they had both religion and trade in common. Later this couple moved to Ephesus, where we shall meet them again (in chap. 5; their expulsion from Rome will be discussed in chap. 6).

Paul preached in the synagogue as long as possible (Acts 18: 4-17). Then he simply moved his activity next door, where a "God-fearer" provided him a new base of operations. This move certainly did not end tensions with the Jewish community. Nonetheless, the presiding officer of the synagogue became a Christian and, according to 1 Corinthians 1:14, was one of the few whom Paul himself baptized. Evidently the relationship with the Jews deteriorated, for Paul was brought before Gallio, charged with undermining Judaism. When the case was dismissed, the accusers vented their wrath on Sosthenes, the new head of the synagogue. Had he encouraged the attempt to have Paul arrested? If he was the same Sosthenes who was with Paul later in Ephesus (1 Cor. 1:1), he would have had an interesting story to tell.

The first converts, according to 1 Corinthians 16:15-18, were Stephanas' household (mentioned also in 1 Cor. 1:15 as one of the few baptized by Paul himself). First Corinthians 16 also mentions names with Latin endings. Were these people descendents of the colonists from Italy? They evidently had enough means to travel, for later they were in Ephesus, when 1 Corinthians was written. From Corinth, the gospel spread to the rest of the province of Achaia (1 Cor. 16:15), and probably northwestward on the mainland as well, as Romans 15:19 suggests. We hear of another congregation in Cenchreae, the eastern harbor on the isthmus (Rom. 16:1).

We do not know why Paul ended his work in Corinth. According to Acts 18:18-23, he left for Ephesus (across the Aegean), Caesarea, Jerusalem ("the church"), and Antioch—but no reason is given for such a trip nor anything further said about it. In any case, the next center of work was Ephesus (discussed in chap. 5). Here, we simply note that while Paul was in Ephesus his difficulties with Corinth began.

Struggles to Save the Church

Paul regarded the developments in Corinth as endangering the integrity of the church and the gospel. Part of his problem was that many of the Corinthians did not see it this way; in fact, they came to look down on Paul and his preaching. Could an apostle in absentia save his own church by writing letters in which he argued, cajoled, explained, and poured out his heart? Before the struggle ended, successfully from Paul's angle, it would take more than letters. But the letters are all that we have, and it is from them alone that the story must be pieced together.

In Ephesus, Paul learned that there were men in the church at Corinth whose sexual habits he regarded as inconsistent with their participation in Christ. So he wrote a letter asking the Corinthians not to associate with such persons (1 Cor. 5:9). This letter is lost, although it has been suggested that a piece of it is now found in 2 Corinthians 6:14—7:1. (This section does interrupt the discussion, but it does not seem to say what we expect the lost letter to say.) In any case, the letter was misunderstood and Paul had to make clear later what he really means (1 Cor. 5:10-13).

Later, the church in Corinth wrote a letter to Paul asking his advice concerning sex and marriage, food which had been offered to the gods before being sold, gifts of the Spirit, and the offering for the poor in Jerusalem. (This list of topics is based on the repetition of the phrase, "Now concerning . . . " in 1 Cor. 7:1, 25; 8:1; 12:1; 16:1.) This letter probably was brought by the persons mentioned in 1 Corinthians 16:17. Presumably they also reported that the previous letter was misunderstood, and carried Paul's reply (1 Corinthians) back to Corinth.

But Paul also had other visitors from Corinth—"Chloe's people," who reported that there were factions in the church (1 Cor. 1:11-12). Evidently the congregation's own letter to Paul did not mention factions! Thus Paul had three sources of information

81

about what was going on in Corinth: the letter from the church, conversations with the delegation which brought the letter, and information supplied by the servants of Chloe.

Paul also learned that some were thinking that he would not return and were stepping into his shoes. Not so, says Paul; he will come soon and show that he is still in charge (1 Cor. 4:17-21). But he did not rely on the letter (1 Corinthians) alone; he had already sent Timothy to visit all the churches in Greece on the way to Corinth (1 Cor. 4:17; 16:10-11; Acts 19:21-22). However Paul was not sure how Timothy would be received. After all, he was a "stand in," and a young one at that (so we may infer from Acts 16:1-3). First Corinthians was written in the winter, probably of A.D. 53-54. Paul planned to go to Corinth after Pentecost.

Apparently neither 1 Corinthians nor Timothy were received well. When word of this reached Paul, he changed his plans and went to Corinth to confront the situation head-on. This too was a failure, and later he wrote of it as a "painful visit" (2 Cor. 2:1). Someone apparently openly opposed him and seems to have had considerable support (2 Cor. 2:5-11). Things had deteriorated because outsiders had arrived who disparaged Paul and his gospel, and promoted their own version of Christianity.

Paul was humiliated, but before leaving he warned them that his next visit would be even more intense (2 Cor. 13:2). After returning to Ephesus, he wrote an anguished letter (mentioned in 2 Cor. 2:3-4). If part of this is preserved in 2 Corinthians 10—13, as is likely, then we see him use sarcasm to attack the outsiders and those who were influenced by them.

But Paul changed his plans. (This too was held against him, 2 Cor. 1:15-17). Now he persuaded Titus, who had been with him at the Jerusalem Council (see p. 60), to be his trouble-shooter and go to Corinth on his behalf. They planned to rendezvous at Troas (=Troy). When Titus did not arrive, Paul, tormented by anxiety, left for Macedonia to meet him (2 Cor. 2:12-13). Upon finding him, Paul was overjoyed to hear that things had settled down. So he sent Titus back to Corinth again; the letter he took is now found in the first part of Second Corinthians (perhaps 2 Cor. 1:1—2:13; 6:11; 7:2-16; 9:1-15). Paul himself arrived later, and the reconciliation was consolidated.

Now Paul decided that his work in this part of the world was done. Next he would take the gospel to Spain! But first, he had to keep his word: he must take the offering for the poor to Jerusalem. Before embarking, he found time to write his greatest letter—the Epistle to the Romans (Rom. 15:22-24). This time, when he said "Farewell!" to the Corinthians, it was for good.

Since we are concerned primarily with the questions which the early Christians had to work through, this chapter will concentrate on First Corinthians.

THE CLASH OF PERSPECTIVES

Before Paul answered the letter from Corinth, he dealt with the factions there. The precise nature of these groups is not clear, but apparently some cliques formed in the name of leaders (Paul, Apollos, Peter), while others disdained all human authority and claimed to belong only to Christ (1 Cor. 1:11-12). Paul is not at all flattered because there are persons who are loyal to him; consequently he does not try to strengthen their hand. Rather, in 1: 13—4:21 he undercuts the basis on which factions arose in the first place.

Paul regards the situation as a symptom of a fundamental misunderstanding of the gospel. To grasp his way of handling it we must see what the Corinthians were thinking.

The Corinthian Standpoint

There were several factors at work. One was Paul's place in the eyes of the congregation. The fact that he had baptized a few of them was one issue. The Corinthians thought they were especially linked to whomever baptized them. Moreover, those who became Christians after Paul left may not have known him at all, except by hearsay. Besides, the misunderstood letter shows that Paul did not always make himself clear. Nor was he as eloquent a speaker as others (1 Cor. 2:3-5; 2 Cor. 10:10). Evidently Apollos, who came from Ephesus (Acts 18:24-28), was more impressive. Also, doubt about Paul's return led to a power-play (1 Cor. 4:18-19).

Finally, they remembered that Paul had not taken any fees but had supported himself and accepted money from the Philippians. The Corinthians, however, were used to seeing traveling teachers and lecturers charge fees. Evidently they viewed fees for lecturers the way people today view fees for doctors: the higher the charge, the better the surgeon. In this light, Paul was an amateur. Paul found it necessary to explain that he had a right to a living from offerings, but had deliberately decided not to take them, lest people think he was taking advantage of them and give the impression that the gospel was a commodity (1 Cor. 9). His explanation did not persuade them, for later he had to deal with the matter again (2 Cor. 11:7-11).

When we put all this together, we see that after Paul was off the scene, some compared him with others and concluded that he was not so impressive after all, while others took up for him and thus polarized the church. The situation was not unlike that in many churches today, especially after an unusually able pastor leaves for another post.

A second factor was Paul's own preaching, especially his emphasis on the Spirit. Every baptized Christian received the Spirit, the divine power. Life "in Christ" or "in the Spirit" (virtually two ways of saying the same thing) was a basic theme of Paul's. For Paul the Spirit was the pledge of salvation, like "earnest money" in real estate (2 Cor. 1:22; "guarantee," as in the RSV, is misleading). He also speaks of the Spirit as the "first-fruits" (Rom. 8:23), from the Old Testament custom of giving the first of the harvest to God as a token of the whole which is to ripen shortly.

In other words, Paul emphasized the Spirit, but he saw it as a reality which pointed ahead to the coming of salvation when the Lord returned. The Spirit is the pledge of the future.

The Corinthians, on the other hand, regarded the Spirit as evidence that they were already saved. They saw themselves as "spiritual persons" who enjoyed the gifts of the Spirit, especially the ability to speak in tongues. They were proud of their Spirit-filled existence. But, as we shall see, this led them to think poorly of Paul, who evidently did not seem "spiritual" enough for them, especially when compared with others. In other words, one of the emphases of Paul's own preaching was being used against him.

The third factor was the theological standpoint from which the Corinthians understood the Spirit, namely, a drift toward an early form of Gnosticism. The terse description of Gnosticism in chapter 3 (p. 74) spoke of certain Christian gnostic teachers who blended belief in Jesus as the Savior with a mentality which regarded this world and its creator as evil. Here we need to sketch a bit more fully the gnostic mind in order to see the extent to which the Corinthians were moving in that direction.

Many ideas which became important to Gnosticism had been around for a long time. Besides, Paul himself believed some of the same things. For example, when he wrote, "flesh and blood cannot inherit the Kingdom of God" (1 Cor. 15:50), every gnostic would have agreed—and a lot of other people as well. What separated Paul from gnostics, and from the Corinthians, was the consequences of this statement.

The gnostics would have concluded that only the soul would inherit the Kingdom, and that this would happen when the soul escaped the prison-house of the body. Paul, however, concluded that "we shall all be changed" so that this mortal body would become immortal, something to occur when the Lord came (1 Cor. 15:51-53). For Paul, both body and soul would be saved because the whole person would be transformed.

Gnosticism, in other words, was a religious movement which insisted that the essence of a person—the soul or spirit—was eternal, but now trapped in the body, which makes it drowsy, drunk, forgetful, and deluded (these are their words). To be saved from this plight, the soul needs knowledge *(gnosis)*. Some gnostic systems taught that a divine savior was sent down into the universe to bring this knowledge. Those gnostics who were Christians said his name was Christ. Some of them said that this divine Christ descended on Jesus at baptism, so that for three years there was a "Jesus-Christ" on earth; just before his crucifixion, the divine Christ abandoned the human Jesus. After all, a divine being cannot die, can he?

The idea that the soul and body are hostile to one another produced two lifestyles. Some concluded that the evil body and its drives must be denied. Others concluded that since only the soul could be saved anyway, one should fulfill the body's drives to demonstrate the point. Both conclusions were being drawn in Corinth.

Paul's Gospel

Paul confronted all factions alike with the center of his gospel —the cross of Christ. When the logic of the cross is understood, there can be no cliques because this logic destroys the basis for forming them. To show what he means, Paul contrasts the cross with "wisdom." The wisdom which the Corinthians prized was not prudence or insight; rather, it was the deeper meaning of things, including the gospel. It is this yearning for deeper meanings, hidden from the ordinary believer, that put them on the road to Gnosticism, whose esoteric explanations (i.e., the gnostic explanation of Jesus' baptism) were offered as wisdom. It "explained" what really happened, and those who understood this felt 'superior to the rest. The clever person who could teach such wisdom was honored because he satisfied the thirst for subtle and mysterious meanings.

Paul lumps all this together and calls it "the wisdom of the world" (1 Cor. 1:20). More important, God saves persons by the message of the cross, which this wisdom regards as foolishness. Surely salvation does not depend on what God did by means of an execution! Yet it does! If this is the case, then what people regard as foolish is really God's wisdom, and what people think is wisdom is shown up as foolishness.

85

The cross means that God has exploded the criteria by which people think about God and themselves. To back this up, Paul points out that if worldly criteria were valid, the Corinthians themselves would never have become Christians because by these standards they were "nobodies" (1 Cor. 1:26-31). Since his preaching, by which they became Christians, did not meet the standards of wisdom which they now use (1 Cor. 2:1-5), they are actually undoing the basis of their salvation.

What has all this to do with the factions? The Corinthians think that since they are spiritual people, they must have spiritual wisdom; so they group themselves around those persons whom each clique thinks measures up best. But in grading their leaders they use the criteria of the world and its wisdom. Factions exist only where people think that particular persons or points of view are better than the rest. Factions continually point out that their leader is better—he can pray better, speak in tongues more often, or produce more subtle explanations than the others.

But the very effort to show such things means appealing to worldly wisdom and criteria which the cross has exposed as foolishness. Factions, party strife, jealousy and the like exist only where the standards of worldly wisdom prevail. The Corinthians think that they are now "spiritual," but their behavior shows that they are very "fleshly" indeed (1 Cor. 3:1-4). Paul does not deny that there are differences among leaders; but he insists that each has his role to play for the good of the whole church and that it is God who makes it thrive, not human achievements (1 Cor. 3:5-9, 21-22).

The arrival of the outsiders apparently destroyed whatever impact First Corinthians may have had. Second Corinthians 10—12 shows that these "false apostles" encouraged the Corinthians to look down even more on Paul. In responding, he plays their game—but with biting sarcasm.

Paul says, in effect, "You want me to boast of my credentials. Well, here they are. I am as much of an apostle as they are. I have more evidence that I am Christ's man than they do, for I suffered more. [He turns their argument around and boasts, not of his accomplishments, but of his vulnerability.] I have had visions and revelations too, but of course I wouldn't know whether I was "in" the body or "out of the body" when I had them. [They evidently regarded their visionary and charismatic experiences as proof that their souls had left the body behind and made contact with the Spirit.] And to keep my feet on the ground, I have this 'thorn in the flesh' [nobody knows what this was], and I can report that my prayer that it be removed was not answered."

Now Paul breaks out of his sarcasm to score his point: "the 'answer' I got was, 'My grace is sufficient for you, my power is made perfect in weakness.'"

Whereas the interlopers boast of their manifest power and achievement, Paul "boasts" of his weakness, for the cross helped him to see that precisely when the world judges him to be "weak" there he is "strong" because God is bringing salvation through such a person. The opponents imply that the effectiveness of the gospel is tied to what one can show of power and achievement. But Paul insists that this kind of thinking cancels the gospel and makes it into nothing more than another piece of religious propaganda.

Interestingly, the current church page of the morning paper illustrates precisely the Corinthian perspective. It contains a huge ad announcing the arrival of a "spirit-filled" Bible teacher, who works with all nine gifts of the Spirit. Come and see, it implies, that he is "more spiritual" than the pastors whose small church ads are dwarfed by this splash. Such thinking would have been very much at home in Corinth.

SEX AND SALVATION

The relation between religion and sexuality has never been simple or uniform, even in Christianity. Ever since the gospel entered the Greek world it has had to struggle for a proper understanding of the body, not just because it is part of the material world but also because its drives make one acutely conscious of conflicting values. Of course, bodily drives and appetites, like hunger or sex, were just as powerful among Semites as among Greeks. But in the West it has been the Greek mentality which has made both a moral and a philosophical and theological problem out of this fact. This is because one strand of Greek culture took for granted a fundamental dualism, a tension, between matter and spirit, the temporal and the eternal, body and soul. Hebrew culture recognized these differences but did not trace them to a clash of incompatible entities, like fire and water, as did the Greeks.

The more pessimistic Greco-Roman thinking became, the more necessary it was to explain why persons partake of both entities, and how soul and body are related to each other, indeed, whether their present relation to one another is the proper one. Clearly, if they are not rightly related to one another now (that is, if the body dominates the soul), then salvation must correct it. Otherwise, it would not be salvation at all but only a religious pain reliever.

Since sexuality involves one of the most elemental aspects of the body, any view of salvation had to deal with it. It is inevitable, therefore, that this question should have arisen at Corinth too.

Conflicting Theologies of the Body

We have already learned enough about the Corinthian outlook and the drift toward gnostic thinking to know how the Corinthians will approach the question—they disdained the body. For them, salvation was the release of their eternal, immortal, intangible souls from the temporal, mortal, tangible bodies. But how could they think this way when the message to which they had responded was Paul's preaching of the cross and resurrection?

As a matter of fact, Paul asked this question too. After reminding them of what he taught and they had accepted, he asked, "Now, if Christ is preached as raised from the dead, how can some of you say there is no resurrection of the dead?" (1 Cor. 15:12). There is no reason to think that they denied life after death. To the contrary, they assumed their eternal souls were immortal and had been awakened to salvation by knowledge of Christ and that being baptized into him guaranteed it. At death their souls would be released from the body and return to God, instead of having to be imprisoned in another body, and so on indefinitely. (Belief in the transmigration of souls, or reincarnation, is normally part of this way of thinking.)

They rejected resurrection because this implies transfer to another body, another prison, and that is no salvation at all. Real salvation is release from every sort of body-prison. For the Corinthians, denying resurrection did not mean forfeiting the gospel; rather, it was grasping the real meaning of salvation. We do not know how they interpreted Jesus' resurrection. There is no evidence that they denied it outright. Probably they relied on "wisdom" to explain it as the release of his eternal soul.

The release of the soul (or spirit) from the body can also be experienced now, especially in intense religious experiences, such as ecstasy, tongue-speaking, and visions. In the present, one will show his or her salvation by the way one treats the body and its drives. Paul and the Corinthians had no argument over the maxim, "Become what you are"—that is, make real and manifest day by day what you really are. They differed radically, however, because Paul could not agree with them on what they were—saved souls. Paul had to make his understanding clear because somebody told him of a situation in Corinth which brought the issue to a head. It was the tip of the iceberg.

According to 1 Corinthians 5:1-8, a Christian man has married his step-mother. What was going on? It is a mistake to blame the city ("It was that kind of town!"); nor should we attribute his action to his moral weakness, still less blame her for seducing him—even if all these things might have been true. Paul is just as hard on the church as he is on the man (evidently she was not a Christian, for he ignores her, in keeping with this policy stated in 1 Cor. 5:12), because they approve of this arrangement instead of taking disciplinary action.

In light of what we have seen, it is clear that these people were showing that they were saved from the body and that what they did with their bodies in no way affected their soul-salvation. They might also have reasoned, as did later gnostics, that laws and customs which restrict sexual activity represent the authority of the creator of this world, and that whoever is really free from the world can (or must) ignore (or deliberately violate) such laws. They might even have appealed to Paul's contention that Christ has made us free from the law (Gal. 3:23-25), and that they were only carrying out the implications of this. In any case, this man was acting out the freedom which was grounded in this view of the body and soul, and his action was putting into practice what others were thinking. That's why they were proud of him.

Paul's response is twofold. First, he asks that the church ratify his decision that the man be expelled (1 Cor. 5:3-5; exactly what v. 5 means is not clear). Second, he expounds an alternative theology of the body (1 Cor. 6:12-20).

In 1 Corinthians 6:12 modern versions put two sentences in quotation marks: "All things are lawful for me" and "Food is meant for the stomach and the stomach for food." The translators have seen that Paul is quoting slogans being used in Corinth, and then answering them. Without the quotation marks, the phrases become Paul's own ideas, which he then counterweighs—a strange procedure. Since the first slogan is repeated in 1 Corinthians 10:23, we shall deal with that in chapter 6; here we examine the second slogan.

What has the slogan, "Food is for the stomach . . ." got to do with sex and body? Evidently the Corinthians were using it to argue that sex organs exist to be used and that we have sexual drives so that they might be fulfilled, not frustrated. Paul does not deny the slogan, but he argues with what it is made to justify, namely that having sexual relations is merely a matter of the body and does not affect the soul at all. Sexual relations, they contended, no more affect the soul than eating does. It is a mere body function, and everyone knows that the body is excluded from salvation precisely because it is a material thing.

The heart of Paul's response asserts exactly the opposite, and must have fallen upon the Corinthians like a bomb: "the body is for the Lord and the Lord is for the body" (1 Cor. 6:13). To the Corinthians, the Lord is for the soul or spirit only. Paul grounds his view in the implications of Jesus' resurrection: God raised him up and will raise us up too. Paul will show in chapter 15 that resurrection is the transformation of the whole person, including the body, because salvation is pledged to the whole self.

For Paul, "body" is not an outer shell which the soul will slough off, even less a prison to be escaped. Rather, body is the external self, the tangible, weighable aspect of the self. This is why he continues, "Do you not know that your bodies [your whole selves] are members of Christ?"

Paul sees a person as a body-soul unit and not as a combination of incompatible components. He says some rather surprising things about the sex act. If body and soul together constitute the person, then sex is not something one does with the body only, but an act which involves the whole self. Intercourse joins persons, not merely bodies. Sex unites selves; it is not simply copulation. Therefore, he infers, even sex with a prostitute joins persons. How can one who has become part of Christ's body turn around and make himself one with a prostitute? (1 Cor. 6:15-16).

Moreover, the experience of the Spirit is not a foretaste of the final separation of the spirit from the body. Rather, receiving the Spirit means that now the body is the temple of the divine Spirit, the place made holy by God's presence. Having the Spirit is not justification for disregarding or despising the body, but precisely the opposite. Having the Spirit means that the body is now a shrine. It is no longer a profane "thing" but a sacred place. "So glorify God in your body!" (1 Cor. 6:20). One can well imagine that the Corinthians made big eyes when this was read to them.

Paul as Marriage Counsellor

Apparently it is Paul's fate to be misunderstood repeatedly. This he experienced already in his lifetime. A century ago he began to be accused of turning the simple message of Jesus into a complicated religion of salvation. Today, it is common to blame him for the narrow view of marriage said to characterize Christianity, and for the exclusion of women from the ministry.

None of these views of Paul stands up, especially when he is seen in his own time; and he can hardly be blamed for what people made of him later. Actually, his views of sex and marriage were rather "down-to-earth"—which may be one reason the Corinthians preferred those with more "wisdom" to offer.

The questions about marriage which the Corinthians put to him (1 Cor. 7) show that not everyone approved of the man who married his step-mother. In fact, others were drawing just the opposite conclusions from the same view of body and soul— that if one receives the Spirit one must deny the body. One cannot have the Spirit and have sex as well. But what if people are already married? And what about cases where only one spouse is a Christian? What should an engaged couple do? And what about widows—should they remarry?

To appreciate Paul's handling of these questions we need to see the angle from which the Corinthians asked them. Above all, we must not judge either the Corinthians or Paul by our own views of marriage—the romantic idea that marriage is based on love and that it must bring both persons a sense of fulfillment. This is a modern, middle class view of marriage. To expect to find it in Paul or in Corinth is as foolish as to expect them to have sponsored a Scout troop.

We know, of course, that also in antiquity there were marriages characterized by love and loyalty. Yet this was more likely to have developed after the ceremony than before. It is, however, as difficult to generalize about the state of marriage then as it is today—and for the same reasons: the situation was changing, and different attitudes existed side by side.

By the time of Paul, women in the Greco-Roman world were far more independent than they had been. Some were prominent in business. Roman law permitted them to sue for divorce, and the legal and economic rights of divorced women were considerable. On the other hand, beside the long-standing honor of marriage there arose a clear contempt for it among some of the Stoic-Cynic philosophers. They appealed to men, asking them to live rationally, not to give in to emotions or be too deeply involved in domestic matters which detracted them from living according to reason.

Whether honored or disdained, marriage was commonly regarded as a necessary institution, needed for raising children and transmitting property in an orderly way.

A second factor in the situation was the tradition, cultivated especially by the gnostics, of regarding the feminine as the weak and passive, and the masculine as the strong and aggressive. Sometimes, evil was associated with the feminine, the emotional, and the material, whereas the masculine is immaterial, reasonable and spiritual. Gnostics took up the old myth that the first human was bisexual (androgynous) but had, for reasons which the myths explained, become divided into male and female. This was regarded as a basic tragedy of human existence. Some Christian gnostics therefore taught that Jesus had said, "I came to destroy the works of the female."

It is unlikely that these ideas were being taught in Corinth already in Paul's time. Yet, they would certainly have been understood, and perhaps accepted, because they had been in the blood stream of Greek culture for a long time. Besides, Paul himself might have known them in some form. At least he believed that salvation overcomes the difference between male and female: "in Christ there is neither male nor female," just as there is "neither Jew nor Greek, slave nor free" (Gal. 3:28).

Paul meant that these differences are no longer as important as people thought, not that they no longer existed. But the language shows that the male-female distinction was taken for granted as a religious question, not merely a biological or sociological one.

A third factor was the vitality of the tradition of asceticism, self-denial for the sake of religious and spiritual concentration. Although asceticism and dualism can reinforce one another (one can deny himself because his body is evil), they are not identical. Fasting, sexual continence, and other forms of self-deprivation have been practiced for centuries by persons who never worried about the relation of the soul to the body. They simply knew that attending to the body distracted them from concentrating on the things of the spirit. Especially the sex drive had to be mastered, it was believed, because this was regarded as lust, a lower animal instinct. The idea that sex can be a beautiful thing which enhances mutual love is a modern idea.

These ways of thinking were in Corinth before Paul arrived. It is therefore easy to see why Christians there would have questions about sex and marriage, especially since they believed that the Spirit made them Spirit-persons, partakers in the realm of the divine in a new, more intense way. The more "spiritual" they were, the more of a problem the body was.

It was probably inevitable that they misunderstood Paul's way of speaking about the flesh and the Spirit. He spoke from a Hebrew standpoint, but they heard it with Greek ears. For Paul, "flesh" was not simply the material prison, the body. Rather, "flesh" stands for body when it dominates, when it becomes the horizon of one's world. Body becomes "flesh" just as creation becomes "this world" when it ceases to be seen as God's creation and becomes a world of its own. Then one lives "according to the flesh."

Then "flesh" becomes a realm of power, something controlling persons.

When Paul speaks of the tension between flesh and Spirit (e.g., Rom. 8:1-11), he did not think in terms of a conflict between two incompatible component parts of the human being, the higher and the lower instincts, but of the conflict between the power of this age and that of the age to come. But the Corinthians understood this as tension between body and soul. As a matter of fact, Paul has been (mis)understood this way most of the time.

Paul's response to the Corinthian questions about sex and marriage is both practical and theological. We saw part of the theological in connection with 1 Corinthians 6:12-20; now we turn to 1 Corinthians 7:26-31. Here Paul does not discuss the Greek view of body and soul, but explains the situation in which Christians find themselves. He refuses to deal with the question in the terms they would have preferred, and makes them play in his park. His point is that there is not much time left for this world because the coming of the Lord was not far off (1 Cor. 7:29, 31). Christians are living in a "lame duck" situation. Soon they (body and soul together) would be transformed (1 Cor. 15:35-57). How are they to act in the meantime?

Paul's central theme is that they should not make the present any more important than it ought to be; it has no future. So one should neither cling to it nor insist on changing it right now. The married should stay that way, the single stay single, the slaves remain slaves, etc. because none of these aspects of the human situation any longer determines one's standing with God or relation to other people in Christ. When he says, "let those who have wives live as though they had none" (1 Cor. 7:29) he is not encouraging them to "sleep around" or to neglect family responsibilities, but to avoid being preoccupied with the family. He makes the same point with respect to business.

Paul's "conservatism" (his council not to make changes) comes from his conviction that the nearness of the Lord makes all present social arrangements of secondary importance at best. It does not come from a belief that the present order reflects God's will and must be preserved. If it was inevitable that Paul was misunderstood with regard to flesh and spirit, it was equally inevitable—though no less unfortunate—that when the church lost its sense of the nearness of the Coming, Paul was taken to argue for keeping things as they are indefinitely.

But this stands Paul on his head. The starting-point of his view is not the permanent, inherent rightness of society as we know it, but its impending end. Paul is not really "conservative" at all; he is finding a way between repudiating this world because it is evil and preserving its present form as if it were divinely-willed. Either position makes the world as we know it more important than it now is.

Paul's practical counsel begins by agreeing that "it is well for a man not to touch a woman" (1 Cor. 7:11). This too may be a slogan used in Corinth (and should be put in quotation marks).

In any case, although Paul agrees that it would be good if people renounced marriage as he had (1 Cor. 7:7), he advises against this because not everyone can master the sex drive. So actually, everyone should be married. Paul relies more on his sense of reality than on a theory of marriage, or on a theoretical view of what the Spirit should be able to do for everyone. This comes through repeatedly as he takes up one particular problem after another.

In marriage people give themselves, including their bodies, to one another. Neither one should deny sex to the other, except for special times of prayer—and then only by mutual consent and for a brief period. One's self-control should never be overestimated. Above all, prayer should not become the excuse for withholding sex.

But suppose the husband or wife is not a Christian. Is it a sin to have sex with an unbelieving spouse? Of course not! There may be domestic difficulties in mixed marriages to be sure, but the Christian should Christianize the marriage if possible, not break it up. If the unbeliever asks for a divorce, let it be. Married Christians should not divorce; but if they do, there should be no remarriage (1 Cor. 7:10-16).

Here Paul recognizes that he cannot be legalistic about Jesus' words because, after all, Jesus never had to deal with these problems. So Paul distinguishes carefully his own counsel from the words of Jesus (1 Cor. 7:10, 12, 25). Paul is striving to be faithful to the meaning of Jesus' words without sentencing Christians to total and literal compliance with them.

He prefers that widows not remarry, but if they do they should marry Christians (1 Cor. 7:39-40). Although in certain cases it may be better for the engaged not to marry, normally it is wiser for them to do so. In any case, marriage is no sin (1 Cor. 7:36-38, also v. 27). In fact, it is not getting married that may lead to sin.

Compared with other attitudes toward sex and marriage at the time, Paul's view is remarkably positive and characterized by a sense of reality—even if it is not romantic and even if he reckons with only the man's sexual drives.

ORDER AND FREEDOM

Must one choose between order and freedom? Freedom, including Christian freedom, is often thought to be opposed to order. Does not order imply a restriction on freedom to do and say as one pleases? Must not movements of liberation and freedom oppose "the old order" which they find repressive? Do not representatives of order feel threatened by assertions of freedom? It seems self-evident that one must indeed choose between freedom or order because one cannot have both at the same time.

On the other hand, there is a long tradition which holds that without order there is no freedom at all but only anarchy. Freedom and order must be balanced—at least stand in tension, it is claimed, because order without freedom is repressive just as freedom without order is chaotic. Questions about the relation of freedom to order became acute in American life in the turbulent 60's, although they have always been there. No society or community exists for long without them.

In the church, questions of order and freedom have sometimes arisen as a struggle between office and Spirit, between clergy (of whatever rank) and persons claiming the power of the Spirit, between the authority of the institution and the authority of inspiration. Since inspiration puts one in touch with the divine, those who have visions and ecstatic experiences (including, sometimes, a "call to preach") do not see any need to be legitimated by merely human authority. They have authorization from God's Spirit.

The possibility for conflict is especially strong when persons in authority also claim to be inspired. Then one must appeal to something else in order to determine whose authority is to prevail. Theoretically, one could decide to follow the person whose inspiration was clearest, strongest, and most manifest. If this could not be determined adequately, the content of what is claimed to come from inspiration could be judged by what is reasonable or useful. Or one could simply fall back on the general standing of the person in the church. In practice, all of these criteria are used.

Paul dealt with these issues in Corinth. Many Christians there emphasized the experience of the Spirit, something for which Paul is doubtless responsible, at least in part. Now those who reveled in the Spirit were challenging Paul, who also had visions and ecstatic experiences. But his response to the factions had closed the door to one way of settling the question of authority—he had refused to play the game of "I am more inspired than you are" because that was a very "fleshly" way of thinking of the Spirit. When he boasts of his religious experiences he does so with deliberate sarcasm and is clearly uncomfortable doing so because he knows he could easily be misunderstood again (2 Cor. 11:16 —12:13).

So Paul must rely on other considerations to establish his authority among the charismatics. But how can he do so without minimizing what he regarded as important—the presence and power of the Spirit? He himself had relied on a vision of the risen Lord to argue that his apostolic authority was equal to that of the Judean apostles who had lived with Jesus (1 Cor. 9:1). He cannot minimize the Spirit without diminishing the basis of his apostleship.

In this section we shall see how he handles these problems. He deals with them in 1 Corinthians 11—14 which is concerned with the congregation assembled for worship. It is here that the freedom of the Spirit became most manifest.

Freedom of Women Prophets

There is a simple reason why Paul cannot be indicted for denying ordination to women—in his churches there was no ordination, period. Only Acts 14:23 could be taken to imply that there was, but generally scholars suspect that here the author reads back into Paul's time the situation of his own generation. First Corinthians shows that in Paul's churches the pattern of leadership reflected the way the gifts of the Spirit were distributed (1 Cor. 12:4-11). (At the same time, Paul assumes throughout that his apostleship gives him paramount authority.) Paul took for granted that the gifts of the Spirit were given also to women.

Women were prominent in Paul's churches (Rom. 16:1, 3-4; 1 Cor. 1:11; Phil. 4:2-3). Acts mentions the names of women who, doubtless, were remembered because they had been prominent in the church (Acts 16:1-15; 17:12, 33; 18:1-3, 24-28). Detailed information is lacking, but the same is true of most of the men. 1 Corinthians 11:4-5 shows as clearly as possible that Paul assumes that both men and women pray and prophesy in church.

The clearer the general picture becomes, the greater is the problem created by 1 Corinthians 14:34-36, which says that women in the Corinthian church should remain silent as they are in all the churches. It is hardly possible that Paul wrote both of these passages in the same letter. Many scholars are therefore persuaded, rightly I think, that 1 Corinthians 14:34-36 was inserted later by someone who agreed with 1 Timothy 2:11-15, written at least one generation later by Paul's disciple. Here too, Paul has had to take the blame for what was said in his name.

It is not clear, unfortunately, exactly what the women prophets were doing in Corinth. In fact, Paul's response is not clear either (1 Cor. 11:2-16). The whole discussion has to do with covered and uncovered heads while praying or prophesying, and it seems that the women were not covering their heads. Paul, however, insists that they do so and looks for reasons to support the demand.

Why would Paul insist on this? Normally Greek women did not cover their heads while praying, although Jewish women did so. It is doubtful that Paul was trying to introduce a Jewish custom into a largely gentile church, as has been suggested. More likely is the suggestion that the women were asserting their right to pray with uncovered heads (like the men) because like the men they were prophesying in the power of the Spirit. In other words, "no veils" became a symbol of equality in the church. Unfortunately, we do not have their interpretation, only Paul's muddled response.

None of the arguments he gives is based on Christian considerations, although verse 3 sets up a Christian authority structure (God is the head of Christ, Christ is the head of the man, the husband is the head of the wife. But where does that leave the unmarried woman?) Verses 11-12 seem to dissolve this, however, since here Paul implies that in the Lord husband and wife belong to one another, as if equals. Paul himself seems to realize that these many attempts to argue the case are going nowhere, so he ends by saying that this is the way he wants it and this is the way all churches are doing it (1 Cor. 11:16).

Paul simply assumes that women must look different from men when prophesying. He feels strongly about this even though he cannot think clearly about it. Fortunately, he never said that it is wrong for a man to cover his head or for a woman to uncover hers. The whole discussion has to do with what is "proper" (v. 13).

In light of what we have observed here, we can say that Paul recognizes that he cannot appeal to the Spirit in an argument with the Spirit-filled women. When he tries to appeal to biblical and biological reasons, this will not work either. So he simply asserts his authority. In any case, he puts no restrictions on the women's right to pray or prophesy in church.

Church Supper and Lord's Supper

We noted in chapter 3 that originally there was no sharp distinction between common meals and the Lord's Supper. People in the Hellenistic world, where sacred meals had been known for centuries, took for granted that the god was present on such occasions, especially when the meals were eaten at the shrine (Paul mentions this practice in 1 Cor. 8:10). Some of the mystery religions (see p. 17) taught that one actually ate the god and thereby received divine power. As noted in chapter 1 (p. 17), people in antiquity took for granted that sacramental acts (eating, washing, anointing, touching) really did something, actually transmitted divine reality. It is doubtful whether anyone in antiquity would have understood the statement, "It's only a symbol."

To understand the problems which Paul saw in Corinth we need to bear in mind also the social situation. The congregation met in the houses of the wealthier members where larger groups could be accommodated. First Corinthians 11:21 implies that the meals were not potluck affairs in which people shared what they brought. Rather each family or circle of friends ate what it brought, so that the poor had little and the wealthier had more than enough. The fact that some got drunk shows that wine was used in ample amounts. It had long been regarded as the sacred drink.

Furthermore, Christians assembled on Sunday, probably in the evening. In those times, Sunday was just another work day in Corinth, and a general 5 o'clock quitting time was unknown. It was difficult, therefore, to know exactly when everyone would arrive.

The social setting reinforced the religious understanding of the meal and produced the problems which Paul tried to correct. The Corinthians believed that the sacred meal made them participants in Christ. Paul believed this too, for in 1 Corinthians 10:16 he asserted that this eating and drinking is a "participation" in the body and blood of the Lord. Evidently the Corinthians concluded that since this is the case, it does not matter whether everyone was there or not. Each group enjoyed the sacred meal whenever it was ready.

Paul, however, regarded this procedure such a profound misuse of the Supper, that he said, "it is not the Lord's supper that you eat" (1 Cor. 11:20). They certainly thought it was. Paul, though, saw that this is not really a common meal which unites the Christians into one congregation, the body of Christ, as it ought to. In 1 Corinthians 10:17 he said, "Because there is one loaf, we who are many are one body, for we all partake of the same loaf." But when each group eats whenever it is ready, the people are not united, and the meal "is not for the better but for the worse" (1 Cor. 11:17) because it accentuates the social and economic differences to the detriment of the poor.

Only when persons of diverse social standing become one body is this really the Lord's table. Paul's counsel in practical: These meals should not be feasts; families can eat and drink as they please at home. Also, they must wait until all have arrived so that they can become one body (1 Cor. 11:33-34). The separation of the Lord's Supper from the church supper begins here.

To undergird his counsel, Paul reminds them of the tradition of the Lord's Supper (1 Cor. 11:23-25). Since First Corinthians was written ten to fifteen years before the Gospel of Mark, this is the oldest written account of the Lord's Supper. In verse 26 Paul adds his comment: every time this meal is eaten, the church proclaims the Lord's death (in the past) until he comes (in the near future).

At the table, the church remembers and hopes. Paul implies that this remembering ought to bring the church together because in the statement "this is my body which is for you," the "you" is plural, as in y'all. Whoever remembers that Christ died for the community will not humiliate the poor by eating the supper as if it were a collection of family picnics under the same roof. What the Corinthians are doing actually profanes the body and blood of the Lord even though they think very highly of it (1 Cor. 11:27).

Paul is interested also in what it means for the individual participant. He calls for self-examination lest anyone participates casually, without being aware of what the body and blood of the Lord really mean. Whoever does so, does not take salvation into himself but judgment. This meal has so much power that Paul attributes the sickness and death of some to the fact that they ate it improperly. Holy things can hurt a person if they are misused.

The Corinthians evidently understood the meal to be a matter of celebrating only salvation; the danger was past. For them the Lord was only the savior, but for Paul he is also the judge, the one to whom Christians are accountable. One must not take salvation for granted, even at the table, for then it is no longer the table of the Lord who is the judge (1 Cor. 11:27-32).

In contrast with Paul's counsel about the veils, his exhortations about the Supper are penetrating and fruitful. He does not question the sacramental understanding of the meal, but shows how it must be understood and observed properly. When this occurs, the body of Christ *at* the table will rightly discern the body *on* the table.

Ecstasy and Responsibility

We have seen again and again that the experience of the Spirit caused the troubles in Corinth. The church itself realized this and asked Paul for guidance (1 Cor. 12:1 begins in the same way as 7:1). In 1 Corinthians 12—14 Paul speaks to the matter directly, having touched on it throughout the letter.

Probably each Sunday evening (1 Cor. 16:2) there was a meal; only after the Lord's Supper became a separate event did Christians worship without this celebration. The Spirit of the risen Lord was present (1 Cor. 5:4), and ecstasy was common. It makes no difference whether we speak of this experience as enthusiasm (or inspiration) or as ecstasy because these words speak of the same experience from two points of view. "Enthusiasm" (or inspiration) means that God has entered the person with power, whereas "ecstasy" means one's spirit stands outside the body in order to enter the divine environment. Either way, the unusual, otherworldly reality controls the self.

The Greek world had many religious groups which enjoyed such experiences. It was not uncommon to compare the divine in-breathing with playing the flute. Just as the flute plays only what is breathed into it, so the enthusiast says and does only what he or she is compelled to. "The Spirit made me do it!"

What the Spirit caused the Corinthians to do was a variety of things. Some received power to heal, others to speak forthrightly and insightfully, others to speak in tongues, and some to interpret what had been said in tongues (1 Cor. 12:8-10). Sometimes they created hymns and prayers (1 Cor. 14:26), sometimes they had visions and heard voices. Paul himself did all of these (1 Cor. 14:18-19; 2 Cor. 12:1-4, 12).

We must try to visualize the situation in which several households were assembled, rich and poor, master and slave, worker and employer together. They sang, prayed, shouted "Amens" to each other's prayers and "Abba!" to God (the Aramaic word for father; Rom. 8:15; Gal. 4:6). "Amens" were common (1 Cor. 14:16). Here sexual and social distinctions no longer mattered (therefore eating in cliques denied the essential meaning). Salvation was real and present, for now they knew that they were in Christ and Christ was in them. Non-Christian neighbors would be invited (1 Cor. 14:22-25) and become part of the Christian community. The meetings clearly lasted more than an hour; they may have gone far into the night.

What, then, went wrong? They began comparing the gifts of the Spirit, and graded them so that some claimed to be "more spiritual" than the rest. They became proud of their gifts, while others felt "second class." Moreover, all these activities were going on at the same time so that the whole scene was bedlam. The larger the congregation became, the more noise they made. This must have bothered some of the Corinthians, because they wrote Paul about it.

Paul's answer shows that he does not want to diminish the place of the Spirit but to put it into perspective. He wants to interpret the whole experience in such a way that it is constructive ("builds up" the congregation, which is what "edifying" means).

He begins by reminding them of their pagan past in order to point out that they had been "moved" before. The experience of ecstasy itself is no criterion of the truth; pagans too have intense, meaningful, "spiritual" experiences. What matters is whether one confesses Jesus to be the Lord; the Spirit never leads one to curse Jesus (1 Cor. 12:1-3).

Did some of the Corinthians really curse Jesus when they were under the influence of the Spirit? This is hard to believe, although it has been suggested that they were so far into Gnosticism that they cursed the human Jesus just to show how much they were part of the spiritual Christ. The solution of the problem depends on whether "Jesus be cursed" is a formula actually used in Corinth, or was Paul's own phrase which he coined to make his point.

Paul next insists that the diverse gifts of the Spirit are from the same Lord and are given for the common good. Each person is an organ (member) of the one body of Christ. It is as ridiculous for a person with an unusual Spirit-gift to look down on another as it is for the eye to say to the hand, "I don't need you." It is as foolish for the person who has a less dramatic gift to say, "I'm not part of this Spirit-filled group" as it is for the foot to think that it is not part of the body because it is not a hand. Rather, this diversity is what makes the whole body. Of course, not everyone has the *same* place and function, but still, there is one body (1 Cor. 12:4-26).

Interestingly, when Paul lists the different roles people have in the church he puts the tongue-speakers last (1 Cor. 12:28), even though he claims he can out-tonguespeak them all (1 Cor. 14:18). Putting the gifts of the Spirit in a descending order allows Paul to urge the readers to seek the higher ones (1 Cor. 12:31).

The most important gift is love, for without it the one who seems to be so much amounts to zero (1 Cor. 13). Paul's celebration of love's perfections can stand on its own, but it is important to see how it functions here. One reason the Spirit was so highly prized was that it is the power of the divine; therefore it is immortal and permanent. The ecstatic experiences come and go, but in them one participates in the eternal. Few things are more Greek than this yearning for the timeless, for what is permanent. The following lines of a hymn are as Greek as they can be:

Change and decay all around I see,
O Thou who changest not,
Abide with me.

The modern American celebration of change would have horrified Greeks because they took change to mean instability and death. That change means progress is a purely modern view, probably based on carefully selected evidence. In any case, given the Greek passion to lay hold of the unchanging (or be grasped by it), it is remarkable that Paul puts the gifts of the Spirit (prophecy, tongues, knowledge) into the category of what passes away. Only faith, hope, and love transcend change, and of these the greatest is love. That must have startled the Corinthians.

Finally, Paul shows why prophecy is better than tongue-speaking (chap. 14). Prophesying is inspired speech which is intelligible to everyone; it need not be a prediction. Tonguespeaking, however, is by definition not speech in ordinary language but in otherworldly speech, "the tongue of angels." (Acts 2 implies that the apostles spoke other languages. This is not how Paul understands "tongues," however.)

Prophecy is better than tongues because it builds up the church, for it is directed toward other Christians. Tongues benefit only the speaker. They cannot build up the church unless they are interpreted. Moreover, a house full of tonguespeakers will make visitors conclude that these people are all out of their minds. But prophecy, being speech which makes sense, can convince guests that God is really present as power (1 Cor. 14:1-25).

What do these distinctions mean for the actual way the Christians are to worship? In 1 Corinthians 14:26-37 Paul answers this with a number of specific exhortations.

—The basic one comes first: everything is to be done for the sake of edifying the church. The worship of the church is not to become a tournament of the Spirit where each competes for the distinction of being the most spiritual.

—There should be no more than three who speak in tongues, and they must not do so at the same time.

—If no one is there who can make sense of what they say in tongues, they should be silent and speak only to themselves and to God. Paul does not believe that a person is so carried away that one cannot keep quiet when it is prudent to do so.

—Two or three prophets should speak, also one at a time, and the others should assess what they say. Paul believes that the prophet is responsible for what he or she says. "The spirits of the prophets are subject to the prophets" (v. 32—another thing which must have offended some of the Corinthians).

How can Paul, himself a Spirit-gifted person, say such things, put such restrictions on Spirit-filled persons? That, doubtless, is what the Corinthians also asked. Paul even suspected how they would react, for he ends by saying that anyone who thinks he is spiritual should know that this command comes from the Lord!

One cannot read this letter without being grateful to Paul for enriching us at so many points. It is in First Corinthians that we have the oldest account of the Lord's Supper and of Jesus' resurrection, the hymn to love, and a considerable body of practical counsel still worth pondering—not to mention Paul's own theological insight. Without First Corinthians our knowledge of earliest Christianity would be immensely poorer. For us, it is also fortunate that the situation in Corinth deteriorated even more after this letter was received, because this development elicited from Paul an even more penetrating exposition of the gospel in Second Corinthians.

We know little of Christianity in Corinth in the decades after Paul. At the end of the second generation, apparently after a period of stability in which the church prospered, factions erupted again. News of this reached the church in Rome, whose leader (Clement) wrote the Corinthians a letter in A.D. 95-96. After praising the church for its magnificent history, Clement speaks of rivalry, strife, anarchy, jealousy, disrespect for elders, and immorality (1 Clem. 3). Clement is not sure how the letter will be received, and he hopes that the three-man delegation will convey the concern of the Roman church (1 Clem. 63).

It all sounds so familiar! If only we could interview these men when they returned to Rome! Their story might be as fascinating as the one Titus told to Paul in Macedonia (see p. 82). Unfortunately, we do not know that story either. What we do know is that the church in Corinth was a remarkable one, whose problems allow many of us today to feel quite at home there.

Chapter Five
THREATS TO CHRISTIAN FREEDOM

Rugged, mountainous Asia Minor (now Turkey) was Paul's bailiwick. Here he was born (in Tarsus, in the southeast), and here he spent most of his life. By his time, the Romans had built a network of roads which made it much easier to cross the many mountains. The western part of the area had been part of Greek civilization for centuries. Many small cities dotted the area.

In the largest and most important city, Ephesus, Paul established the center of his mission. It was the capital of the province, and had been a major harbor. Already in New Testament times, however, the harbor was filling with silt; eventually it could no longer be used. Still the old city continued to thrive; after all, it was then already a thousand years old. It was here that the goddess Artemis (whom the King James Version calls Diana) was worshipped for centuries. Her temple was considered one of the seven wonders of the world. In Paul's day, the stadium was being rebuilt, as was the magnificent amphitheater on the western slope of the hill. Here too there was a strong Jewish community.

PAUL'S BASE IN EPHESUS

According to Acts, the church here was not actually founded by Paul, though doubtless he gave it definitive shape. The original nucleus was the husband-wife team with whom he became associated in Corinth—Aquila and Priscilla (Acts 18:18-19). They converted an Alexandrian Jew, Apollos, who later went to Corinth where he had considerable success as a Christian preacher. Although one of the cliques there used his name, Paul did not regard him as an opponent (1 Cor. 1:11; 3:5-9, 21-23; 4:6-7; 16:12). Apollos was a Hellenized Jew (he is named for a Greek God) who, from the perspective of Aquila and Priscilla, had been only half Christianized (Acts 18:25). When Paul arrived later, he persuaded more of such Jews to become Christians (Acts 19:

1-7). No one knows what sort of sect this was, nor do we hear any more of them.

Paul's preaching split the Jewish community when some of them became Christians (Acts 19:8-10). When he lost his platform in the synagogue, he rented a lecture hall, a common practice. Although Paul stayed more than two years, Acts tells us nothing about the new church there. It is interested rather in dramatic encounters.

The story of Paul's confrontation with Jewish exorcists (Acts 19:11-20) makes two points: only Christians can use Jesus' name to expel demons, and Christian exorcism is not magic. The story is not told to encourage book burning. The long story of the riot (Acts 19:23-41) shows there was local anti-Semitism, and that abandoning the religion of Artemis was regarded as disloyalty to the city. The combination of religious patriotism and patriotic religion will be an even greater danger in the second generation, as we shall see.

Why does Acts have no interest in reporting the internal life of Paul's churches? In Acts 20:17-38 (the story of Paul's last contact with Ephesus) we have a clue to an explanation for this. This story marks the end of Paul's entire mission, for now he is on the way to Jerusalem where he will become a prisoner. Actually, the story is only the framework for a long speech (vv. 18-35). Acts regularly uses long speeches at turning-points in order to bring out the meaning of the narrative (e.g., Acts 2:14-36 [Pentecost]; 7:2-53 [Stephen's indictment of Israel and the temple]; 13:16-41 [Paul's preaching to Hellenistic Jews]).

Paul's speech reviews his work and looks into the future (the author's time). Writers often used farewell speeches in this way. Acts 20:29-30 has the clue we mentioned: the church will experience controversies and factions *after* Paul is gone. In other words, Acts is written from the standpoint of the author who, writing for divided churches in the second generation, looks back to the time of Paul which he portrays as free of internal difficulties. In fact, one often has the impression that some of these controversies are over the way Paul is being remembered and used. In these circumstances, the author would scarcely have called attention to arguments over Paul during Paul's life time. That would not have helped to heal the church for which the author wrote.

However, Paul did face troubles in his churches. Paul's letters hint that this was true also in Ephesus. In 1 Corinthians 15:32 he refers to a fight with wild beasts. This should not be taken literally, as if he were in the arena, because he is using a figure of speech, somewhat like "I had a tiger by the tail."

105

In 2 Corinthians 1:8-11 he implies that his troubles were so severe that he expected to die. Did he think he would be executed? Was he in prison? For some decades, scholars have discussed the possibility that he was a prisoner, and a number of things fall into place if we assume he was. For example, Romans 16:3 says Aquila and Prisca "risked their necks" for Paul, something easier to put in Ephesus than in Corinth.

More important, the so-called "prison letters" (Philippians, Colossians, Philemon) are easier to explain if the prison was in Ephesus rather than in far-off Rome, the traditional place. Philippians 1:12-18 says that Paul's imprisonment had a double effect on the church. The majority became all the more "confident in the Lord," but some leaders took advantage of the fact that Paul was "out of circulation" to advance their own standing and to make matters worse for Paul.

From Ephesus, Paul also had to deal with problems in other churches. In chapter 4 we traced his controversies with Corinth. During the same period, he had to salvage the situation in Galatia. He also had to deal with problems in Colossae, including the delicate matter of a runaway slave. When we see the picture as a whole, we understand why he should speak of "the daily pressure upon me of my anxiety for all the churches" as well as of physical suffering (2 Cor. 11:28).

We cannot use the Letter to the Ephesians to learn about the church in Ephesus in Paul's time. In the first place, it is by no means clear that Paul himself wrote it. Many scholars, this one included, are convinced that it was written later by one of Paul's successors. The many reasons for concluding this cannot be discussed here. Two things, however, can be mentioned. Paul would hardly write to a church where he had spent two years and assume that they had only heard of his ministry, as Ephesians 3:2 puts it. Also, Ephesians 4:11 assumes a more advanced form of institutional structure than does 1 Corinthians 12:27-30, where the church is led by the Spirit through its diverse gifts, not through distinct offices as in Ephesians. Even if the letter had been written by Paul, it does not mention specific matters in the lives of the readers.

Ephesus became the center from which Christianity reached the surrounding area. By the end of the century, there were Christian congregations in most cities of Asia Minor. Some of them were addressed by the Revelation to John, and some received letters from Bishop Ignatius ten or fifteen years later (see p. 72). In the New Testament, the congregation in Colossae is the only one of these "daughter churches" to claim to have a letter from Paul. Colossians 4:16 mentions a letter to the congregation in Laodicea, but it no longer exists. The "Letter of Paul to the Laodiceans" which we do have is another one, written in the second century.

In the next section, we shall explore the problems in the Asia Minor churches which Paul addressed while he was in Ephesus. In the third section, we shall note an entirely new question faced by the second generation, especially in Ephesus—persecution by the government. Both situations threatened Christian freedom at the core.

A MANIFESTO OF CHRISTIAN FREEDOM

"Eternal vigilance is the price of liberty." This common saying is as true of Christian freedom as it is of political liberty. Christian freedom is threatened from many sides. One of the most persistent threats comes from the desire of the Christian who wants to do something to improve the salvation he or she already has.

Is it really the case that one is rightly related to God simply and solely by believing the gospel? Surely this is only the beginning. By no means, argues Paul. It is precisely in trusting God on the basis of the gospel that we have all the salvation we can have in the present. In this trust there is freedom from sin. Is this freedom only a transitional stage which is needed before one can get on with doing things that make one a real Christian? Or is this freedom, found in trust, itself the whole point? On this issue Paul and the Galatians collided head on.

The Letter to the Galatians was sent to a group of congregations (Gal. 1:2). Where they were located is disputed, although the traditional view is that they were the churches established during Paul's first missionary trip, reported in Acts 13—14. We do not need to decide the question, but we do need to see what prompted this intense response from Paul. Actually, we mentioned it before (pp. 59-61); here we need to fill in the details, then to grasp Paul's reply.

Circumcision as Perfection

One reason Paul is so agitated is that his understanding of the gospel and his own standing as an apostle are being undermined. Christian Jewish teachers, never identified, moved through the Galatian churches and persuaded the Christians to accept circumcision. Paul regarded that issue settled at the Jerusalem council, and interpreted the Galatian response to the travelers as sheer desertion from the gospel. The Galatians themselves, doubtless, did not understand it this way. Nor is it clear that they thought they were rejecting Paul outright, though he is convinced that this is what is going on.

In reading his letter, therefore, we must not confuse Paul's interpretation with theirs. Nor must we take what Paul says about the motives of the travellers to be a report of how they explained themselves to the Galatians. The whole situation would be much clearer, of course, if we had their side of the story. All we have, however, is Paul's tightly-argued response, and it is from this that we must reconstruct the situation in Galatia.

At the end of the letter, Paul stops dictating and takes the pen himself. Here he denies the integrity of those who have caused the trouble and explains their motives:

It is those who want to make a good showing in the flesh that would compel you to be circumcised, and only in order that they may not be persecuted for the cross of Christ. For even those who receive circumcision do not themselves keep the law, but they desire to have you circumcised that they may glory in your flesh.

—Galatians 6:12-13.

In chapter 3 we used this passage to point to the political dimension of the problem faced by the Jerusalem Council, some years earlier. We suggested that given the rapidly rising Jewish nationalism in Palestine, the Jewish Christians there might have been under pressure to prove their loyalty to the nation by disassociating themselves from gentile Christianity. So long as they were part of a movement which included the uncircumcised, the Jewish Christians in Palestine would be vulnerable to the charge of betrayal from the Zealot-minded. Rather than split the church, some may have reasoned, it is better to have the gentiles circumcised.

The refusal to the Council to require circumcision could only have made matters worse, for now the Jerusalem Christians clearly were involved in a movement which was not fully committed to the nation and the Torah. The stronger the gentile churches became, the more difficult it was for Judean Christians to argue that gentiles were being brought into the true Israel. Instead, the Jewish Christians were becoming a shrinking minority in a religion which regarded circumcision and Jewish practices as mere customs.

What could be done? The Council could not be convened again. Paul was somewhere in Asia Minor; Barnabas was on Cyprus (Acts 15:39), and Peter may have been in Antioch. If the gentile Christians could be persuaded to accept circumcision after all, then the Jewish Christians could report that they had actually enlarged the nation, and this, in turn, might avert persecution. Such a reconstruction is plausible in view of Paul's words and in light of the times.

What would these people tell the Galatians? It is unlikely that they could have gotten them to accept circumcision simply to spare the church in Jerusalem. More important, Paul had not required it when they were baptized. They had to deal with that. Apparently their strategy was to say that Paul had not required it because he wanted to please them, to make it easier for them to be Christians. We may infer this from Paul's sharp counter-question, "Am I now [at the time of writing] seeking the favor of men or of God? Or am I trying to please men?" (Gal. 1:10).

Furthermore, these travelling teachers from Jerusalem argued that Paul had actually conceded that he was subject to Jerusalem by going to the Council in the first place. This explains why Paul insists on his independence from Jerusalem; he was not summoned by superiors but went "by revelation." Besides, the so-called "pillars" acknowledged that his gospel was as valid as that of the others. In fact, he claims, he got it "not from men or through men but through Christ" (Gal. 1:1, 11-12, 16).

The most important question, of course, is how circumcision was being interpreted. Galatians 5:3 insists that everyone who is circumcised obligates himself to keep the *whole* law. Paul bears down on this point because the Galatians had not understood it this way. Evidently the men from Jerusalem had not made this clear. They portrayed circumcision as something necessary for a new level of Christian life. Otherwise, why would the Galatians have accepted it so quickly (Gal. 1:6)?

The clue is in Galatians 3:3, although it is not visible in the RSV: "Having begun with the Spirit, are you now ending with the flesh?" The NEB has ". . . do you now look to the material to make you perfect?" It is not merely a matter of getting sidetracked, of starting in one thing and ending up in another. It is a matter of achieving perfection. In other words, the Galatians had been persuaded that the Christianity which Paul had brought them was only the first level; faith-given salvation is only the beginning. Perfection requires circumcision.

What sort of perfection is this? The answer lies between the lines of Paul's argument in Galatians 3. This chapter is hard to understand because we are listening in on an argument over the interpretation of the Old Testament, and we are hearing less than half of it because everything that has been said before is taken for granted.

Paul's opponents were basing their argument on Abraham, the father of the Jewish people. In Hellenized Judaism, Abraham was the model proselyte who left idolatry (symbolized by Mesopotamia) in order to undertake the journey to perfection (symbolized by his migrations). According to Genesis 17:1, God appeared to him and said, "I am God almighty; walk [live] before me and be blameless." The Galatians, like Paul, read this in Greek, which translated the last two words as "be perfect." Since Genesis 17 goes on to report that the aged Abraham circumcised himself, the chapter could be taken to mean that circumcision was necessary before Abraham reached perfection.

We do not understand why anyone would have interpreted Genesis 17 this way because we see no relation between an operation on the penis and spiritual perfection. But Hellenistic Jews did. We must remember that one of the religious questions which they faced was: How can one make sense of traditional Jewish practices? One did not get very far, either in conversation with Greeks or in private reflection, by answering, "All of us Jews do it," nor by saying, "We do it because the Bible commands these things." Instead, they found symbolic meaning in Jewish practices.

According to the Greek view of matter (flesh) and spirit, the flesh drags down the spirit. The flesh must therefore be controlled because it is the source of passions and lusts. On this basis, they interpreted circumcision as a symbolic act. Cutting off some flesh, especially this flesh, stands for freedom from bondage to the flesh. In other words, the Galatians accepted circumcision because they became persuaded that it symbolized the freedom from the world. Now they could become perfect.

Circumcision as the Forfeit of Freedom

Paul regards the whole development in Galatia as a disaster, because in trying to improve their salvation the Galatians are losing it. The freedom which they have in faith is not a stage on the way toward something better, but is itself the sign of salvation. As he puts it in Galatians 5:1: "for freedom Christ has set us free." One cannot add to this; one can only lose it by trying to.

Before looking at Paul's counter-argument more closely, two comments are in order. First, the theological issue of circumcision is not of only antiquarian interest, something we no longer have to deal with. Paul put it into a broader theological framework which is perennially relevant.

Every religious act by which one expects to gain something from God is a form of "circumcision." Circumcision embodies the question, Does salvation depend on doing something, or simply and solely by trusting God? For Paul, it is trust, and trust alone, that puts one in right relation to God. Salvation is either a sheer gift, or it is some sort of reward for doing required things. It cannot be both at the same time. Whenever someone, the Christian included, undertakes doing something in order to gain salvation (or to improve trust-given salvation, as in Galatia), one actually loses it because salvation by "doing" differs fundamentally from salvation by "trusting."

To understand what Paul is really fighting for, we need to ask what form "circumcision" might take today. What are the supplementary requirements people sometimes place on Christians if they want to become "real Christians?" Theologically it does not matter what these requirements are. Whoever advocates requirement is a modern Galatian.

The second comment flows from the first: The argument over circumcision does not concern only men. Theologically women can be as much caught up in "circumcision" as men, because this operation stands for reliance on doing in order to be really Christian. No one is a bystander as Paul battles for Christian freedom.

Paul's counter-argument is so tightly reasoned that summarizing it makes it even harder to understand. We shall be content, then, to note certain key points in Galatians 3.

First, if the Galatians would think clearly about their own Christian experience, the salvation which they have by faith (or trust), they would see that circumcision does not add anything, but cancels what they already have. On the one hand, when they trusted God on the basis of the gospel they were baptized and received the gift of the Spirit. The freedom and power of the Spirit, the life of salvation, is what they want most. Fine. They already have it. Did they receive the Spirit because they obeyed the law (which accepting circumcision implies)? If that were the case, Christ is irrelevant because the law has been available for centuries. If they have the freedom of the Spirit already, then surely they do not need circumcision to acquire it or to get more of it.

On the other hand, if flesh and Spirit are indeed in tension— Paul does not deny this because for him Spirit is God's gift, not human spirit, the higher self—then how can an operation on the flesh bring a gift from God? Paul simply refuses to discuss whether the Hellenistic Jewish view of circumcision is valid, because he is talking about God's Spirit not human spirit.

111

Second, Paul agrees that Christians are heirs of Abraham. The question, however, is, What makes one an heir? The Galatians had been persuaded that faith alone did not suffice for this, and circumcision was needed in order to be "Abrahamic." Because Paul's opponents were arguing from the Scriptures, Paul must show that they misinterpreted it. In doing so, he brings to light a distinctly Pauline view of how law and gospel, Judaism and Christianity as ways of salvation (not as religious communities) are related.

There are several aspects to Paul's interpretation of the Scriptures here.

• Evidently Paul's opponents were arguing that Christians must repeat Abraham's experience (see p. 110). Paul agrees, but then he explains what that really was. He observes that God had already pronounced Abraham to be righteous before he circumcised himself (Gen. 15:6), and that God had done so because Abraham believed God and trusted him. Abraham's standing with God could not depend on later circumcision; neither does that of the Galatians. Furthermore, at the outset of the Abraham story, in Genesis 12, God promises that the gentiles would be blessed through (or, in) Abraham. The opponents, of course, read this too, and concluded that the important thing comes last (circumcision and perfection in Gen. 17).

Paul, however, argued that the important thing comes first (in Gen. 12). Just as a will is not annulled or changed by later events, so the later law of Moses, which requires circumcision, does not cancel the original arrangement with Abraham: faith (alone) establishes the right relation with God. Precisely in order to be "Abrahamic" one does not need circumcision.

• If the law does not override the covenant with Abraham, why did God give it in the first place? "Because of transgression" (Gal. 3:19). That is, sin made the law necessary in order to make life tolerable and to restrain sin. It was not an advance over Abraham, nor a permanently valid set of requirements for salvation. It was a temporary relief measure, now superseded.

To illustrate, Paul compares the law with a trustee or guardian (Gal. 3:24; the RSV has "custodian" but this is misleading because it suggests a janitor). The word has also been translated "tutor" but Paul is not claiming that the law educates us toward Christ. He is speaking about the law as the non-permanent authority over children, like that of guardians. In Christ, people are free from the law because they are now "of age."

Whoever is circumcised therefore falls back into this old bondage because circumcision puts one under the whole law (Gal.

5:1). Circumcision is not an advance into perfection at all; it is a relapse. Law is now outmoded because sin and flesh can really be dealt with in Christ. Whoever takes up circumcision is not buying into the future; after Christ, the law is an Edsel.

• Gentiles do not become heirs of Abraham by individual circumcision. To show this, Paul reads Genesis 17:12 like a lawyer who builds his case on the exact wording of a contract. He notes that the promise to Abraham speaks of his "offspring" (literally, "seed"). This, he concludes, means there is only *one* heir—Christ.

What has this to do with the Galatians or any other gentile? Everything. They were baptized into Christ, made participants in the one heir. They are already Abraham's children. In Christ "there is neither Jew nor Greek, there is neither slave nor free, there is neither male nor female; for you are all one in Christ Jesus. And if you are Christ's then you are Abraham's offspring, heirs according to [on the basis of] the promise," not on the basis of circumcision. In Christ, the believer is a child of Abraham precisely because one is free from the law.

This mode of argument might seem strange to us, but Paul was a man of his time and it was common to use Scripture this way.

Third, Paul argues that freedom from the law does not mean that one is free from all restraint against sin and flesh. By "flesh," Paul means human nature in rebellion against God, not sheer physicial existence. Rebellious existence must be dealt with indeed. But the law could not do so. It actually makes one conscious of sin, as Paul explains to the Romans (Rom. 3:20).

The law could not give real life; only the Spirit can do that (Gal. 3:21; Rom. 8:2-4 develops this). Flesh is dealt with only by death—that is, to die with Christ, or as Galatians 5:24 puts it, "those who belong to Christ Jesus have crucified the flesh with its passions and desires." What the law is really after—humane life in society—is fulfilled in love of neighbor (Gal. 5:14). This love is the primary result of the Spirit; it is not an achievement. Whoever lives by the Spirit which the Christian already has, does what the law is all about—yet does so as a free person, not as one in bondage to law.

Just as we can be grateful to the Corinthians for creating crises which evoked from Paul his ever-deeper exposition of Christian life, so we can be thankful to the Galatians for provoking Paul into writing this manifesto of Christian freedom. A few years later, he developed these themes in the Epistle to the Romans.

113

CHRISTIAN FREEDOM WITHOUT FEAR

Studying about amulets and horoscopes can be a lot of fun. Christians, at any rate, can scarcely take them more seriously than Hallowe'en—at least if they believe what the Letter to the Colossians has to say. Should we be especially cautious every time Friday falls on the 13th of the month? Not if this letter is right. Do the stars really control events on earth? Is this world so dangerous a place that one needs charms to ward off evil influences the way some people used to wear asafetida bags to keep sickness away? Should a Christian use such things—just in case? Not if the Epistle to the Colossians is on target. Who runs this world anyway?

We are not the first to ask such questions because we are not the first to be afraid of the world, to fear claiming the full range of Christian freedom. Whereas Christian freedom in Galatia was threatened by influences on earth, at Colossae it was threatened by invisible powers. After all, freedom in Christ has its limits, doesn't it? The Colossians thought so.

The Invisible Power Structure

Paul himself did not take the gospel to Colossae, a city inland from Ephesus. Apparently it was a Colossian, Epaphras, who introduced the gospel there after Paul had won him to the Christian faith. Later, when Epaphras was again with Paul he reported problems which had arisen in Colossae. Shortly afterwards, he was a fellow-prisoner with Paul (Philemon 23). Although some scholars think this prison was in Rome, probably it was in Ephesus.

A much more important question is whether Paul himself wrote the letter. Scholars are far more divided on this question than they are about Ephesians. The complex evidence cannot be discussed here. We will simply observe that the close connection of the letter to Colossae with the Letter to Philemon, which no one doubts is from Paul, makes it likely that Paul wrote both. The Letter to the Colossians might have been expanded later, but that too cannot be discussed here. The letter to Colossae responds to problems which do not seem to have been introduced by outsiders, as was the case in Galatia. These problems were home-grown, but that did not make them less pressing.

The Colossians assumed that the world is a dangerous place, not because of robbers, disease, or war, but simply because it was the world, governed by invisible powers. This view was common in the Greco-Roman world. It represented a blend of certain Jewish ideas and practices with old pagan ones, some of which can be traced to ancient Mesopotamia and Persia. People in Asia Minor, having been ruled by Persians, Greeks, and now Romans, encouraged the fusion of different religious beliefs and practices. Probably the Colossians took such ideas for granted long before they became Christians. The question was not, Shall Christians adopt the horoscope? but rather, What shall we do with our horoscope now that we have become Christians?

We do not know, of course, that the Colossians actually consulted their horoscopes seriously; "horoscope" is a convenient symbol for the drift of things in Colossae. By this time, we expect to find some gnostic elements along with other things. However, whereas many gnostics were hostile to Judaism, the trend in Colossae combined Jewish elements with gnostic ones, gnostic beliefs and Jewish practices. How did all this hang together?

First, they viewed the universe the way most people did—the earth was the center, and around it revolved the planets in concentric circles. It was their interpretation of a universe constructed

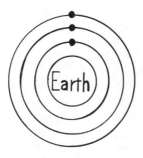

this way which was decisive. They believed that the heavenly bodies were the homes of invisible powers who are hostile to humans.

If the foregoing diagram is understood to be a view from the "top," so to speak, then it simply shows the relative distance of each planet from the center. But it the diagram is understood as a view from the "side," then some planets are "higher" than others. Since it was assumed that influence flows downward, it was clear that the "higher" planets influenced the lower ones, and that earth is influenced by them all. To be on earth is to be subject to the entire power-structure. The human situation is like a prison which is surrounded by many rings of hostile guards. This view of the self and the universe is basic to Gnosticism, but one did not need to be a gnostic to think this way.

These invisible powers had many names. Even in the New Testament, there is considerable variety:

angels	Rom. 8:38; Col. 2:18
authorities	Eph. 1:21
dominions	Eph. 1:21
elemental powers	Gal. 4:3; Col. 2:8, 20
powers	Rom. 8:38; Eph. 1:21; 6:12 Col. 2:15
principalities	Rom. 8:38; Eph. 6:12
rulers of this age	1 Cor. 2:8

These names appear in various combinations; consistency does not really matter. They are the "world rulers of this present darkness," the "spiritual hosts of wickedness in the heavenly places" mentioned in Ephesians 6:12.

Because the human body is made of matter from the earth, which is subject to all these powers, the powers control people. The powers administer fate. As the relation of one planet to another changes, the nature of the influence changes too. In other words, astronomy was really astrology. The more people knew about astronomy, the more clear it seemed that the whole universe operated by the laws of fate, and that earthlings were its victims. Ancient people had long believed in fate (and in good fortune or luck), but scientific knowledge of the planets and stars made the whole universe into a prison run by unchangeable laws.

In the second place, in order to make life tolerable one had to learn how to cope with the situation. There were several things one might do. One could counteract the influence of the powers by knowing precisely how they operated; that is, by magic one could force them to work for you instead of against you. Or, one could respect their special interests, such as certain days or times. Or, one could actually worship them—that is, simply acknowledge their power.

The calendar was of special importance. No one knows how old is the idea that each day of the week is the special province of each of the seven planets. In any case, the seventh day was under the control of Saturn, the largest and "highest" of the planets; we still call it "Saturn-day." The first day was "Sun-day" while the second was "Moon-day." For centuries people had been fascinated with the moon, especially because of its 28-day cycle; "lunatic," we remember, is a word for a person who becomes insane by the influence of the moon *(luna)*.

We must not expect to find a single, coherent set of beliefs and practices. What we find is a great variety in emphasis and practice.

In such an environment Jews used some of these ideas to emphasize the Sabbath, and gentiles believed that mysterious-sounding Jewish words had special magical power, and borrowed them whenever they could. Whatever the "mix" might have been in a particular situation, the whole thing expressed the belief that human life is the victim of hostile powers who rule the universe.

In the third place, the letter to the Colossians was addressed to Christians involved in this kind of thinking. The Colossian Christians had come under the influence of a "philosophy" (Col. 2:8), or a teaching, which claimed to explain all these things. Such things fascinated the Colossians—and some moderns as well! The teachers of this "philosophy" also advocated measures for dealing with the powers. These included observing special days and taboos (Col. 2:16-18, 21), perhaps circumcision as well (Col. 2:11).

How could the Colossians, being Christians, have accepted such ideas? On the one hand, as said already, many of them probably believed them to start with. On the other hand, they must have been told that faith in Christ did not go far enough; one still must deal with these powers. It is hard to learn just what the Colossians came to believe about Christ himself. One thing, however, is clear—as they understood matters, the coming of Christ did not really bring any changes in the universe or in the way people are related to it. Probably they thought that Christ brought salvation for the soul when a person died, but that in the meanwhile, there are these powers to contend with.

At first, what the Colossians were into may seem strange to us. Yet, similar views of the world are held by Christians today, even by those who have no interest in fate or horoscopes. It is not uncommon to find Christians who are convinced that there is an invisible power structure which manipulates everything and everyone. Nowadays too it has all sorts of names. Sometimes the names are abstractions, recognized by words that end in -ism: communism, capitalism, fascism, imperialism. Sometimes more concrete names are used: Mafia, military-industrial complex, the establishment (sometimes "eastern," sometimes "liberal," sometimes both). Whatever the name, the point of view is always the same: good, innocent people (the speaker) are victims of a worldwide conspiracy and therefore must find ways to cope with this "spiritual wickedness in high places" because one cannot really change it. Salvation is rescue from this tyranny, and Jesus is the one who made this possible for the believing individual. But not even he changed anything.

117

Christ the Head

Paul did not contest the Colossian view of the universe, nor did he argue that really there are no principalities and powers. He too believed these things. Therefore his letter develops his thinking within this framework. Paul's response has four aspects: the nature of Christ and the meaning of his death and resurrection; the proper way of regarding the cosmos and its powers now; the meaning of baptism; and the appropriate way of dealing with what is "earthy" in us. We shall look briefly at each of these.

First, because Paul too believes that the planets revolve around the earth and that there are hostile powers, it was natural that he taught that the divine Son of God descended into the cosmos to become Jesus on earth. His saving work done, the risen One ascended; he left the cosmos and entered God's presence. This descent/ascent pattern was common to Hellenistic Christianity's understanding of Christ. The descent of the Son expresses the incarnation in terms of space, and the ascent expresses his vindication and glorification.

The earliest use of this pattern is found in hymns such as Philippians 2:5-11; John 1:1-18 (minus vv. 6-8, 15 which are prose), and Colossians 1:15-20. Scholars recognize that these hymns are probably older than the texts in which they are now found. Some modern translations do not print them in poetry however, because there is still some uncertainty about the exact length of the stanzas.

In other words in Colossians 1:15-20 Paul quotes an early hymn and comments on it. (It is not necessary here to distinguish the hymn itself from Paul's comments, which seem to be inserted into it.) The hymn is relevant to the Colossian situation because it asserts that "in him [Christ, the Son who "pre-existed" before he became Jesus] all things were created"—that is, the Son entered his own universe. The powers belong to him to begin with; he created them. They became hostile, apparently, by some sort of rebellion. How or why this occurred is never said in the New Testament. Second century gnostic theology explained all this in great detail.

The event of Christ ended the rebellion because the cross and resurrection defeated the powers (Col. 2:15) and so reconciled the whole universe to God (Col. 1:20). Paul interprets the execution and resurrection as a power struggle whereby God's Son regained sovereignty over his own creation. (Evidently the re-assertion of sovereignty is still underway; at least 1 Cor. 15:24-28 makes this clear.) Jesus' resurrection raised him to God's "right

118

hand" as Colossians 3:1 puts it. Paul explains what this means:

Christ is now "above" all the powers; he is "the head of all rule and authority" (Col. 2:10). The powers do not yet acknowledge this, but that does not change the truth of the matter.

Second, for the Christian who knows this and participates in Christ, the powers hold no terror. They have been dehorned. If Christ is now Lord, nothing in the cosmos has the last word, and need be feared (Rom. 8:35-39 says this too). Christians are not to regard themselves as victims of the world or to act as if they were. Christ is the Head of the body, the church (Col. 1:18; 2:19), and the Head of the church is at the same time the Head of the universe. Believing in Christ does not make Christians aliens in the world; rather, they are the first to be truly at home in it.

The concern for special days, special taboos and the like, is now outdated. As far as the influence of the "elemental spirits of the universe" is concerned, Christians are as good as dead—the powers cannot affect them any longer. Christians can ignore all the paraphernalia developed to cope with the powers. As Colossians 2:20-21 puts it, "If with Christ you died to the elemental spirits of the universe, why do you live as if you still belong to the world? Why do you submit to regulations, 'Do not handle, Do not taste, Do not touch'?" The world is no longer the dangerous place it once was; it belongs to its rightful Head once more.

Unfortunately, this emphasis on the lordship of Christ led to Christian imperialism, especially after Christianity grew to be the official religion from the fourth century onward. If the Head of the church rules the world, then the church can try to rule the world in the name of Christ. Paul, of course, could not foresee such a development, and should not be blamed for it. In his day, the lordship of Christ gave Christians freedom, not mastery.

Third, by baptism persons become participants in the new administration (Col. 2:12). Being put under the water incorporates one into Christ's death, and emerging from it makes one participate in his resurrection so that one is "raised with Christ" (Col. 3:1).

Paul speaks somewhat differently about baptism here from the way he does in Romans 6:1-11. There he also says that baptism unites the person with Christ's death, but he seems to avoid saying that one has already participated in Christ's resurrection. Rather, this is still future: "we shall certainly be united with him in a resurrection like his" (Rom. 6:5).

The difference may seem small to us, but in Paul's day it was large because one reason the Corinthians were so arrogant about their salvation was that they believed they already shared Christ's resurrection power and were saved already, and free from danger. This is why Paul writes so sarcastically in 1 Corinthians 4:8: "Already you are filled! Already you have become rich! Without us you have become kings!" This is also why Paul points out that not every Israelite who had been baptized into Moses (at the Red Sea) got to Canaan (1 Cor. 10:1-13).

In fact, what Paul says about baptism in Colossians is so close to what the Corinthians were thinking that many scholars regard this as a good reason to doubt Paul wrote Colossians. It is also possible, however, that Paul emphasized participation in Christ's resurrection when writing to the Colossians because in that situation the point was not dangerous. Since Paul was dealing with the Corinthians at the same time, he may have come to see how easily this point could be distorted, and so shifted his emphasis when he wrote to the Romans later. In any case, Colossians regards baptism as actual participation in Christ's resurrection as well as his death.

Paul therefore writes, "If then you have been raised with Christ, set your minds on things that are above, not on things that are on earth" (Col. 3:1-2). Does this mean that the Christian is to be "other-worldly"? Not in the common meaning of the phrase! In Colossae, what is "above" is above the principalities and powers, not simply "other-worldly." Paul says in effect, "don't be concerned with the powers any more; concentrate on him who is above them." The Colossians should not be concerned with earthly things because observing special days, special taboos and the like is being really quite earthbound.

Finally, Paul agrees with the Colossians that "what is earthly" in the Christian must be dealt with (Col. 3:5), but he interprets it quite differently. What is earthly is not simply what is physical, but what is immoral (Col. 3:5, 8-10). Colossians 2:20 implies that the Colossians were understanding circumcision as a sign of rejecting the earthly, as was the case in Galatia. But here Paul does not argue against circumcision; he says rather that in baptism one rejects what "the fleshly" really means—a distorted way of life. Moreover, all the taboos and regulations mentioned in Colossians 2:20-23 are futile; they cannot deal with what is truly earthly—immorality.

One can paraphrase Paul's point: "You cannot deal with gluttony by forbidding food; you cannot deal with lust by forbidding sex." The way to deal with what is truly earthly (fleshly) is spelled out in Colossians 3:12-17. Again, the most important thing is love.

CHRISTIAN FREEDOM AND THE HOUSEHOLD

Today, we go to church, sometimes after alternatives are discussed, sometimes routinely. In early Christianity, there was no church (building) to go to; instead, the church (congregation) came to the house. Probably it was customary for entire households to arrive because often everyone, including slaves, in the house practiced the same religion as the father (e.g., Acts 16: 33; 1 Cor. 1:16).

In antiquity slavery was simply taken for granted. Ancient slavery differed from that developed in America. For one thing, it was not tied to race. There were, of course, black slaves too, but most slaves came from the same races and peoples as their owners. Slaves, after all, were frequently persons captured in war or kidnapped by pirates; often people sold themselves into slavery. Often the slave had a better education than his owner, and so became the children's tutor. Slaves could earn money and buy their freedom. More and more, masters granted them freedom. In some ways the slave in that time was better off than the black slave in America, in some ways worse. Slave revolts occurred from time to time, and harsh laws were enacted to discourage attempts to escape. Punishment for those who did and were caught could be extreme.

We can easily imagine the sorts of problems which would arise when households became Christian, especially when both the owner and the slave were baptized into Christ. Does this change their relationship? Does it change only during worship, or does it change all week long? Suppose the slave becomes a Christian but his master remains a pagan who regards the new faith as another weird superstition; is the Christian slave to obey a master who sneers at the Lord Jesus? If every Christian receives the same Spirit on the same basis, is everyone equalized? Will the traditional structure of the family be changed by the adoption of Christianity?

Slave, Yet More Than a Slave

Onesimus had run away from his master, Philemon of Colossae. Somehow he met Paul, who won him to the Christian faith. Onesimus, in turn, became one of Paul's associates. This created a delicate and dangerous situation.

After Onesimus fled, it seems, Philemon became a Christian, and perhaps a leader in the congregation. Onesimus seems to have been a poor investment, for Paul says that previously he was useless to Philemon but now he is useful to Paul as well as to Philemon. (*Onesimus* means "useful.") Nonetheless, he is an escapee,

121

hiding from the law; but he is also a Christian. If he returns, what can he expect? Perhaps he should stay with Paul. Doing so, however, endangers Paul, because then the apostle would be hiding a runaway slave—a serious offense, doubly so for a man who is already a prisoner!

This is the setting in which Paul sent a letter to Philemon, whom he may never have met. It is a masterpiece of diplomacy and tact. The letter is actually addressed to Philemon and the house church where he is known. Paul seems to count on the congregation's making it more difficult for Philemon to refuse what he asks—to take Onesimus back as his slave, yet more than a slave.

Paul's reasoning is fascinating. He says he might have simply settled the matter by declaring, if anyone had investigated, that Onesimus was indeed Philemon's slave but that he was now representing Philemon in helping Paul. But, he notes, that would have been rather presumptuous. This point, however, should suggest to Philemon that what he proposes is not the only possibility. In asking Philemon to receive him forever "no longer as a slave but more than a slave, as a beloved brother," (v. 16) Paul seems to suggest that he ought to set him free. Indeed, Philemon ought to welcome his slave the way he would welcome Paul—a free man and Christian brother.

Paul volunteers to pay whatever Onesimus might owe (Had he taken something when he fled?). On this basis, Onesimus need not remain a slave in order to work off his debt. Paul hopes that Onesimus will be received, freed, and sent back to join Paul and his friends. Unfortunately, we do not know what happened. It is tempting to regard Bishop Onesimus of Ephesus around A.D. 110 as the same man. The name is fairly common, however, and probably one should resist the temptation.

Paul, being a man of his time, did not criticize slavery or call for its abolition. We have already seen why he seems to have been "conservative" in such matters (chap. 4, p. 93). Paul's attitude toward slavery appears also in 1 Corinthians 7. In fact, however, 1 Corinthians 7:21 is ambiguous. The RSV translates this advice to slaves as "if you can gain your freedom, avail yourself of the opportunity;" the NEB, however, may give the correct translation in a footnote: "even if a chance of liberty should come, choose rather to make good use of your servitude."

Be that as it may, Paul did not speak against slavery. One wonders whether he would have thought differently about it if he had seen the slaves in the Spanish silver mines and not only household slaves like Onesimus.

Household Duties

The Letter to the Colossians contains one of several "lists of household duties" which are found in the New Testament. These lists resemble Hellenistic moral teaching outside the New Testament. Their common pattern is clear.

Colossians 3:18—4:1	Ephesians 5:21—6:9	Titus 2:2-10	1 Peter 2:18—3:7
wives	wives	older men	servants
husbands	husbands	older women	wives
children	children	young women, wives	husbands
fathers	fathers	young men	
slaves	slaves	slaves	
masters	masters		

Four brief observations emerge from looking at these materials. First, the seven letters which are accepted by all scholars as being unquestionably from Paul do not contain these lists of duties (Romans, 1, 2 Corinthians, Galatians, Philippians, 1 Thessalonians, Philemon). Paul addresses all Christians equally, without distinction. If Paul wrote Colossians, then this would be the first time that he addressed specific counsels to persons on the basis of their place in the household.

Second, some of the advice could have been given to any household at the time; it is not particularly Christian. Fundamentally healthy human relationships are not discerned only by Christians, nor found only in Christian homes. Conversely, Christians have the same fundamental obligations as other people. In other words, these common household responsibilities are made Christian by the motivation of the persons, and by the total context in which life is lived—being in Christ.

Third, what catches our attention today is the command that wives obey their husbands. Then it was probably regarded as self-evident. What might have caught the readers' attention then was the insistence that husbands love their wives.

Fourth, more and more, the attitude of Christian slaves toward their masters comes into view, especially if the masters were not Christians. This is emphasized by 1 Timothy 6:1-2 also. Evidently such situations created tensions. It was one thing to be relatively indifferent to being a slave if the Lord's coming would soon change everything. It was something else to have to live with the indignity some decades later, when the Lord's coming seemed to be postponed indefinitely.

One cannot help but ask why it was necessary to urge Christian slaves not to "pilfer" (Titus 2:10), and why Titus has no word of counsel to give to the masters. One is tempted to conclude that as more and more persons of means became Christians, the church found itself thinking like the masters.

The financial security of Christian widows has a special concern from the beginning (Acts 6:1). Taking care of "the widow and the orphan" had long been a part of Judaism, and Christians continued the practice. For the Epistle of James, taking care of these people in distress is one of the two hallmarks of pure religion (Jas. 1:27). For some reason, financial security does not play a role in Paul's advice to widows in 1 Corinthians 7 (see p. 94). Over the years, apparently, the Christian "welfare program" developed to such an extent, and was subject to so many abuses, that regulations had to be devised.

A set of regulations is found in 1 Timothy 5:3-16, probably written around A.D. 100 or shortly thereafter, which shows us several things. Some families were taking advantage of the church's readiness to help. The strong language indicates that the writer is dealing with real situations, not simply with possibilities: "If anyone does not provide for his relatives, and especially for his own family, he has disowned the faith and is worse than an unbeliever."

Also, by this time "widow" was a technical term, not simply a word for any woman whose husband had died but who had not yet remarried. This is why the writer speaks of being "enrolled as a widow." The church found it necessary to specify just who was and who was not qualified to be registered as a "widow," just as the IRS must specify who counts as a "dependent." Like a modern welfare regulation, 1 Timothy 5 spells out the qualifications: she must be over 60 years old, have been married but once, and have a reputation for charitable deeds (she who is to receive must herself have given aid). This regulation assumes that the woman had not been destitute before becoming a widow.

Apparently, "registered widows" promised to remain unmarried. Therefore young widows are urged to marry and "rule their households." The situation which the writer wants to avoid is clear: young widows, being registered for church support, have time of their hands and so "learn to be idlers, gadding about from house to house." The writer assumes that young widows have no business or professional opportunities. They must either be married, or be supported by relatives or by the church—or else take to the streets. How different is this passage from what Paul himself had to say to widows decades earlier!

LORD JESUS AND LORD CAESAR

No question has vexed Christians more than this one: At what point must one say no to the claims of the state? The conflict between the church and the state has been a persistent theme in the West, and has taken dramatic forms from time to time. Only in Judaism and in Christianity has willingness to be executed played so great a role.

To account for this, one would need to reckon with many factors. One of them is the fact that the central figure in Christianity was himself executed by the state. Also, the universal symbol of this religion is the means of his execution—the cross.

Another factor is the unwillingness of Christians and Jews to give ultimate allegiance to anything other than God—the God, moreover, who cannot be identified too closely with any thing or any person in the world. Unfortunately, governments often put on religious airs. Experience has taught Christians to be sensitive to the religious pretensions and claims of the state. The tuition for learning this has been paid in blood.

The price was first paid in Asia Minor almost 1900 years ago. To be sure, there were martyrs before this. However, Stephen's death had been at the hands of a mob, and Nero's executions resulted from his desire for scapegoats, as we shall see. The religious claims of the state first collided directly with the claims of Christ in A.D. 95.

In the midst of that experience a political exile had a series of visions which unmasked the demonic nature of a totalitarian state with religious trappings. Fortunately, he wrote down what he saw; we know it as the Revelation to John.

The Religious Aura of Empire

What the Constitution of the United States asserts is without precedent—that the state is created by the people for their own good and is accountable to them. The Constitution does not claim that the United States government is God's gift, but a human creation: "We, the people. . . ." In antiquity, the opposite view prevailed. The state had a divine aura about it, and its rulers were taken to be more than human beings. In Egypt the Pharaohs were regarded as the embodiment of the gods. It was common for the successors of Alexander to call themselves Savior, God Manifest, Benefactor, and the like.

Roman religion was essentially cultic patriotism. It was believed that the gods looked after Rome's prosperity and power so long as they were worshipped rightly. The priests were government servants. Participation in religious processions or having the priest offer prayers and burn sacrifices for Rome's sake was not so much a matter of personal piety as of public duty and patriotism. These rites were the thing to do, much as invocations today are used at political conventions, inaugurations, or football games.

Doubtless many persons also felt deeply about Rome and the gods who made her great, just as today some people have a sense of the holy when they sing "God Bless America." But in the main, personal religious needs were met elsewhere, in the mystery cults and in the religious activities of the home.

The religious aura of the empire was carefully fostered by the emperors, largely to legitimate the government and unify the domain. Religious propaganda was put out by some of the poets. This was easy enough to do because the first emperor, Augustus (who insisted that he be called the First Citizen!) brought peace, prosperity, and stability to a war-weary world. The new empire was hailed as the return of the Golden Age, and Augustus was regarded as the gift of the gods.

In the provinces Augustus was actually hailed as a god, a savior. He himself refused to be called a god, but encouraged people to worship his "genius"—the god-given wisdom or spirit which enabled him to achieve what he did. At his death, his successor Tiberius urged the Senate to acknowledge that he was among the gods; from now on, he could be worshipped as one of them.

Repeatedly from this point on, new emperors arranged for the Senate to have their predecessors accorded divine honors. This was a way of showing the government's continuity, as well as respect for the previous emperor.

It is hard to know just how seriously people took all this. The emperors themselves sometimes could be sarcastic about it. Vespasian, on his deathbed, murmured, "I'm afraid I'm turning into a god!" The public worship of the emperor, or of his genius, apparently was a rather routine thing. Refusing to participate, however, was regarded as an affront and as a subversive act.

The issue did not come to a head for the Christians until the reign of Domitian (A.D. 81-96). He insisted that he be addressed as "our lord and god," and he fostered emperor worship as a way of unifying the empire. Apparently in western Asia Minor government officials were especially eager to enforce this patriotic religion. Christians faced a test of loyalty. There seems to have been a brief, but intense, persecution because the Christians, many of them at least, simply refused to participate.

From the standpoint of the government, this Christian refusal was a sign of disloyalty, a self-incriminating act which could not be tolerated if the government was to be respected. The government regarded Christian refusal as treason. From another standpoint, one might say that the Christians were foolish, and unnecessarily stubborn. After all, one might reason, they could have put the incense on the altar without taking it all that seriously. They knew that the emperor is not a god. It's only a gesture. If they had gone along with it, they would not have set a bad precedent.

Perhaps some did think this way. Many, however, did not. For them such thinking was treason to Christ. One of those who were uncompromising must have made enough trouble to be exiled to Patmos, a small island off the coast near Ephesus. There, one Sunday, his visions began.

Reality and Destiny Revealed

The Book of Revelation belongs to that type of Jewish and Christian literature known as "apocalyptic" (the Greek word *apokalypsis* means revelation). Most Jewish apocalypses were produced during the period of oppression and revolt, from 168 B.C. to A.D. 135, although there are apocalyptic passages in earlier writings as well.

Most apocalypses did not get into the Bible, and many of them have disappeared. Among the survivors are books which claim to be written by Adam, Baruch, Enoch, Moses, as well as James, Paul and Peter. The Revelation to John belongs with this literature because it also reports visions about the End, the Last Judgment, the fate of the damned and the blessedness of the redeemed—all of which are found in apocalyptic texts. Since many apocalypses are compilations of earlier writings, it is often difficult to see a clear organization in the book as a whole.

We shall not "explain" the Book of Revelation. Rather, we shall restrict our discussion to two aspects of this fascinating book: the view of the Roman empire which is expressed in chapters 12 and 13 especially, and the picture of the Asia Minor churches which read it first. There are other ways of studying and appreciating this book, to be sure; but here we concentrate on the historical approach. We shall read it in light of the times for which it was written by a man known only as "John."

It is almost certain that the writer was neither the author of the Gospel of John nor a disciple of Jesus—nor does he claim to be. He was a prophet who sent a word of encouragement to the congregations facing persecution for refusing to participate in emperor worship.

Rome: Divine or Demonic? Persons who had apocalyptic visions, as did John, probably were thoroughly at home in apocalyptic literature and traditions. The imagery and symbols of this literature are rich and diverse; many have been traced to ancient Babylon and Persia. The apocalyptists drew on these materials in order to interpret their times, which called for dramatic symbols. The Revelation to John used such symbols to disclose the deeper meaning of the situation of the church in the world.

Fundamental to the apocalyptic perspective is the conviction that the struggles of the faithful on earth are part of a cosmic conflict between God and anti-God, an old motif. In the visionary experience, these invisible heavenly realities become visible so that the seer can interpret what is happening, or is about to happen, on earth. (Apocalyptic writers did not predict events which were to happen centuries later; they dealt with the crises of their own times.)

In Revelation 12—13 John shows the readers that what happens on earth can be understood only in light of what has happened in the heavens. The crisis in Asia Minor is but the local earthly engagement of a cosmic war between Satan (the dragon) and the Messiah and the Messiah's people. In resisting Domitian, he implies, Christians are battling the cosmic forces of evil. This cosmic dimension of the situation explains why the action in these two chapters shifts back and forth between the heavenly world and earth.

Revelation 12 gets our attention first. The theme is cosmic conflict: the pregnant heavenly woman is set over against the heavenly dragon (Rev. 12:1-3). On earth, the dragon's intent to devour the baby (the Messiah) is thwarted because the child is taken up to God (Rev. 12:4-5). Using a baby to symbolize the Messiah brings out the contrast between the helplessness of Jesus (he is also called the lamb in Rev. 5:6) and the brutality of evil. The vision does not refer to "the baby Jesus" but to Jesus' passion and resurrection.

The vision assumes that the execution of Jesus is part of the war between God and Satan, and that Satan used Roman power to attack the Messiah. Revelation 12:13-17 repeats and elaborates the story of Revelation 12:4-6—the church now endures the same hostility which Jesus had endured (it is persecuted).

Revelation 12:7-12 gives the heavenly counterpart to the earthly scene: the dragon is defeated by Michael (the guardian of the saints). The earthly means of this defeat is astounding—Jesus' death and Christian martyrdom. Martyrdom is not defeat but victory. Avoiding martyrdom would be defeat for the believer and victory for Domitian. Why? Because one can avoid becoming a martyr by worshipping the emperor.

It might look like a victory for the emperor's agents to get a Christian to acknowledge that Caesar is Lord. The Christian too is tempted to regard that as Satan's victory because those who refuse lose their lives. Ultimately, however, the opposite is true because Jesus' resurrection has defeated Satan. Christians who lose their lives gain their salvation.

Revelation 13 interprets the same situation, but with different symbols. In apocalyptic tradition, evil emerges from the sea, the symbol of chaos. In Daniel 7, four beasts come from the sea: a lion, a bear, a leopard, and one so dreadful that it cannot be compared with any animal. These beasts represent the sequence of empires: (probably) the Babylonian, the Medean, the Persian, and the Greek. The same theme is expressed in Revelation 13: the beast from the sea is an empire, Rome. Revelation 13:1-2 combines elements of the beasts in Daniel 7 because John believes that in Rome all evils in the past come to a head. This beast receives the dragon's power—that is, Rome rules by Satanic power.

According to Revelation 13:4, people worship the beast, because they are awed by its power. The beast blasphemes God—an allusion to emperor worship in general and to Domitian's claim that he is lord and god, specifically. God allows the beast to persecute the church, but only for a limited time (symbolized by an exact number). In the midst of persecution the church should know that God is in charge, despite appearances to the contrary.

Revelation 13:11-18 introduces a second beast. It compels people to worship the first one. The second beast is the imperial priesthood which promotes emperor worship.

People are often fascinated by the 666 (some manuscripts have 616) mentioned in Revelation 13:18. The number names a person in code. To understand it we need to remember that before the Arabs gave us our numbers, Greeks, Romans, and Jews counted with letters. If we do this in English, then a = 1, b = 2, c = 3, etc. With such a system one can "count" names. For example, Abe = 8 (1+2+5). All sorts of combinations can add up to 666.

Three possibilities are of special interest. We can spell *Neron Kaisar* in Hebrew, and then add up the name to get 666. On this basis, the number would mean that Nero, the evil torturer, had returned, as some thought he would. Or we can add up the abbreviation of Domitian's titles which he put on coins. On this basis, the number refers to Domitian himself. The number 666 might be the evil counterpart to 888, the sum of "Jesus" in Greek. Actually, it is not clear that John had only one meaning in mind.

The exact meaning of details, not only in Revelation 12—13 but throughout the book, remains uncertain. One thing is clear, however: John regards Rome as evil (in chap. 17, Rome is called the Great Whore). John's visions interpret the totalitarian state which he knew. However, the question is whether what he saw does not come true repeatedly, especially whenever a totalitarian state emerges from the chaos of history.

The Book of Revelation does not speak for the whole New Testament. We recall that Jesus' reply to the question about the coin implied a different view (see p. 50). In the next chapter we shall see that Romans 13 says exactly the opposite from Revelation 13. For Paul, the emperor is the servant of God, not the agent of Satan. It is worth pondering whether Mark 12, Romans 13, or Revelation 13 offers the most insight into the question of how the Christian today ought to understand the modern state and one's relation to it.

The Future of the Vulnerable Church. Before John interpreted the danger to the church from outside, he addressed the threats which he saw within it. He did so in seven letters to seven churches in western Asia Minor (Rev. 2—3), beginning with Ephesus (probably his own church; we do not know why Colossae was omitted). The letters are very much alike. They all begin with words of praise for the church's achievements, and then usually call attention to a blemish on its record and issue a warning.

All the churches have a summons to hear what the Spirit is now saying, and a promise of reward for fidelity. Each letter takes account of local circumstances. At the same time, the seven churches stand for the whole church. Our interest here is in what the letters show about the churches of the area at the end of the first century.

The letters give the impression that the churches have prospered and that Christians have garnered considerable experience. Curiously, there is no mention of Paul or of his successors. Instead, we read of persons and groups mentioned nowhere else. It is difficult to learn much about them; usually they are mentioned in connection with some sort of false teaching.

The Book of Acts, it will be recalled (p. 105), reflects internal controversies in the churches in this area. The Book of Revelation, written a decade later, confirms this. John opposes two groups in Ephesus. One is known as the Nicolaitans, who were a problem also at Pergamum (Rev. 2:6, 15). No one knows who they were or what they taught. John regards them as modern equivalents to Balaam and Balak (Num. 31:16; 25:1-3), ancient perverters of Israel. Another group was teaching that Christians may eat food offered to idols. John also accuses them of "immorality" (the word can refer to various infringements of sexual morals).

Why was "food that had been offered to idols" a problem? It was customary to offer the gods part of a slaughtered animal and to sell the rest. It was probably impossible to buy any meat that had not been symbolically offered to the gods—unless one knew a Jewish butcher. Years before, Paul had to face the problem in Corinth, and he wrote to the Romans about it as well (discussed in the next chapter). In 1 Corinthians 8 he agreed with those in Corinth who saw no reason why Christians should not be free to eat this meat because the gods to whom it had been dedicated did not exist in the first place.

Some Christians felt free even to eat meals with friends at the shrines. At the same time, Paul was aware that some people have scruples about the matter, and he counselled that, for the sake of these persons, one should forego eating such food. However, to the Colossians, as we saw, Paul wrote that all taboos about food are now irrelevant. It is possible that some years later, there were groups in these churches who insisted on eating such food in order to make a point of their freedom. In any case, John's response is quite different from Paul's.

The problem of this "idol meat" appears also in Thyatira (Rev. 2:20), where eating it was being advocated by a woman prophet whose name is not known. John simply denounces her as a "Jezebel." Jezebel was the Phoenician wife of King Ahab of Israel nine centuries earlier (1 Kings 16:31; 2 Kings 9:22, 30). She was an ardent worshipper of her gods and the persecutor to Elijah.

To call this Christian prophetess "Jezebel" was to characterize her as a fiendish danger, and to imply that he, John, was an "Elijah" battling for the truth. Evidently she claimed to know deep mysteries, which John regards as the profundities of Satan (Rev. 2:24). He accuses the Christians of committing "adultery" with her (Rev. 2:22), meaning that they follow her teaching, not that they were immoral. She may have been a teacher of some sort of Gnosticism. There must have been a power struggle between her and John, for he says, "I gave her time to repent but she refuses. . . ."

A second problem was a certain slackening of devotion in some of the churches. Even though Ephesus had detected the true apostles from the false, it has lost its first love (Rev. 2:4). Sardis has the reputation of being a live church but to John it is really a dead one (Rev. 3:1). For the Laodiceans, Christian faith has become routine, so that John says they are neither hot nor cold. Like a thirsty person getting tepid water from a drinking fountain, the Lord will spit them out of his mouth (Rev. 3:15-16). Whereas the church in Smyrna is poor but does not know how rich it really is (Rev. 2:9), the church in Laodicea is proud of its wealthy members but does not know how poverty-sticken it really is (Rev. 3:17). Taken as a whole, the churches were a "mixed bag"—exactly as Matthew, John's contemporary, had seen in Antioch also.

A third problem had to do with a Jewish group which is impossible to identify. Revelation 2:9 speaks of slander which Christians in Smyrna endure from "those who say they are Jews and are not." Apparently the same situation is found in Philadelphia (Rev. 3:9). John denounces this type of Judaism as the "synagogue of Satan." Perhaps these Jews were rather thoroughly Hellenized, and participated in emperor worship as a mere patriotic gesture.

A fourth problem concerned the churches' response to the danger of arrest and punishment. Christians in Smyrna face imprisonment (Rev. 2:10). In antiquity this was detention before punishment, not punishment itself. Often torture preceded execution. At Pergamum a certain Antipas had already been executed but the church as a whole had not flinched (Rev. 2:13). Even where this fate is not explicitly mentioned, John encourages the readers who are facing the sort of harassment which minority groups often endure. He writes of patient endurance, tribulation, and the danger of copping out (Rev. 2:3, 9; 3:8, 10).

Some of the churches are called on to repent, others to hold fast. The distinction should not be pressed because the seven churches together represent the whole church. As John sees the situation, repentance will prepare the church for what is about to happen—persecution and martyrdom. The church as it is cannot survive unless it intensifies and purifies its allegiance to Christ.

Repenting means turning from dangers and errors, and holding fast to the confession that Jesus alone is the Lord. He himself was the faithful witness (Rev. 1:5). The word translated "witness" also means "martyr." In Revelation 5, no one but the exalted Jesus is "worthy" to unravel the scroll (the mystery of human existence) because he alone, by suffering, became the Conqueror, the triumphant Lamb. His victory assures the harassed and persecuted Christians that come what may, they too shall prevail.

We do not know how long the persecution lasted, nor how the church actually fared. We do know that it was but the beginning.

Chapter Six

TEMPORAL CHRISTIANS IN
THE ETERNAL CITY

If someone had told the earliest Christians in Jerusalem that a hundred years later the most important church would be in Rome, they would have denounced him as a false prophet. In the first place, they did not think that there would be any churches a hundred years later, for they expected the Lord to have returned long before that. In the second place, being Christianized Jews, they assumed that the center of the Kingdom would be Jerusalem.

However, the Lord did not return as expected, and the War of A.D. 66-70 more or less annihilated the Jewish Christian church in Jerusalem. After the Second Revolt in A.D. 132-135, the small church in Jerusalem was a gentile congregation, since Jews were forbidden to live there. A century after the first congregation emerged in Jerusalem, our imaginary prophet would have been proven right. Jerusalem Christianity was in decline, and the sun was rising over Rome, where the action was.

Rome, to be sure, was not the only major center of Christianity in A.D. 135. Antioch, Ephesus, and Alexandria were key cities in which Christianity was flourishing. Unfortunately, we know almost nothing about the arrival of Christianity in Alexandria, and only a little more about how it came to Rome.

EARLIEST CHRISTIANITY IN ROME

Christianity took root in Rome during the hey-day of the empire. Rome had grown to be a city of more than a million people, many of whom probably lived in cramped apartment buildings which were at least three stories high—something new in the world—and which often collapsed. Many families lived in the single rooms above the small shops.

Except for the suburban villas, the wealthy apparently lived next to the poor, and frequent fires threatened both. Sewerage was a continual problem, despite the numerous public baths and toilets. We would regard most of the streets as mere alleys or passageways, for in contrast with the planned cities founded by Alexander the Great and his successors, the streets of ancient Rome formed no pattern. At night, they were dark, and inviting to crime. So congested was the city that vehicles were banned from the streets during the day. In the midst of the jumble stood the magnificent public buildings.

Wealth flowed to the upper classes while the vast majority of the population grew ever poorer. Indeed, between one-third and one-half lived on public charity. The multimillionaires owned hundreds of slaves, though most households probably had no more than a few. Freeing slaves became common, however, and it has been estimated that by the second century at least 80 percent of the population were freed persons or descendents of freed slaves.

There was a Jewish community in Rome from the second century B.C. onward. Roman Jews apparently never endured waves of anti-Jewish riots, as did those in Alexandria. A great deal has been learned about Roman Jews from their underground cemeteries, the catacombs, several of which have been discovered. It appears that there was no single Jewish quarter in Rome; nor were Jews organized as a single national group with a large measure of self-government as in Alexandria.

Rather, the Jews in Rome were organized as synagogues, which the Romans classified as "associations," each of which apparently had its founder or sponsor. As associations, the synagogues had the legal right to own property and collect funds, some of which were sent annually to the temple in Jerusalem and some of which were used for communal banquets—an important aspect of the many trade, craft, burial, and religious associations. However, synagogues were not allowed within the inner city, the sacred limits of Rome. Only religions officially accepted into the city by action of the Senate could build temples and shrines within the sacred city.

Despite the relatively secure status of Roman Jews, we do hear of several occasions when government action was taken against them. The earliest occurred in 139 B.C., when some Jews were expelled for "trying to corrupt Roman customs"—probably the way Romans understood Jewish efforts to convert their neighbors. Rome did not single out Jews in this regard. To the Roman mind, religious practices were patriotic acts. To tamper in any way

134

with public religious rites, or to dissuade anyone from partici-
pating, was to engage in subversion.

We hear of another move against Jews in A.D. 19, when four
thousand are reported to have been exiled to Sardinia. According
to Seutonius, a second-century historian, the emperor Tiberius
"abolished foreign cults at Rome, particularly the Egyptian and
the Jewish, forcing all citizens who had embraced these super-
stitous faiths to burn their vestments and other accessories." As-
trologers were also expelled, unless they promised to stop making
predictions.

According to Acts 18:2, Aquila and his wife Priscilla arrived in
Corinth as Jewish refugees from Rome "because Claudius had
commanded all the Jews to leave Rome." (The "all" is doubtless
an exaggeration.) This report is supported by Seutonius, who
wrote that "since the Jews constantly made disturbances at the
instigation of Chrestus, Claudius expelled them from Rome" (in
A.D. 49).

Whether "Chrestus" was a local Jewish agitator, or whether
this name was a misunderstanding of "Christ" is not clear. If the
latter be correct, then two conclusions follow: First, Aquila and
Priscilla probably were Chrisitans before they left Rome. Second,
the Christian preaching that Jesus was the Christ (the Messiah)
caused enough controversy among Jews to be noticed by the
authorities. Unfortunately, this is all we know about the Chrestus-
controversy. Scholars generally assume that Roman Jews, returning from Jerusalem where they had come to believe the gospel,
introduced Christianity to Jews in Rome.

There is no reason to doubt, however, that the arrival of Christianity created controversies in the Jewish community. According
to Acts, Paul's preaching in the synagogues of the empire repeatedly generated intense reactions (e.g., Acts 17:1-9; 18:5-8, 12-
17). It is not surprising that, according to Acts 28:22, the Jewish
leaders in Rome tell Paul that "with regard to this sect [Chris-
tianity] we know that everywhere it is spoken against." Here too,
Paul's preaching divided the Jewish community. The author of
Acts regards the Jews' response as a sign that they had rejected
the gospel, for he has Paul apply Isaiah 6:9-10 to this situation
and conclude that from now on the gospel will go to the gentiles.
Actually, this is the third time this point has been made (Acts
13:44-49; 18:5-7). Yet each time before, Paul continued to go
to the Jews first.

Acts regards the rejection of the gospel by the Jews of the
dispersion as the reason the church became predominantly gentile,
and he also believes that this fulfilled the Scriptures. We do not

know the circumstances in which Roman gentiles first became Christian. In any case, when Paul arrived in about A.D. 59, Christianity may have been in Rome for a decade.

Paul did not arrive in Rome a free agent, but as a prisoner intent on presenting his case directly to Caesar (Nero). At least three or four years earlier he had planned to go to Rome, where he hoped to receive support for his mission to Spain (Rom. 15: 22-29). However, he decided that he had to take the offering for the poor to Jerusalem rather than sending it with others. He was uncertain whether it would be accepted, and he may have felt it unwise to let others deal with the situation there. The offering, which had been agreed upon at the Jerusalem Council (Gal. 2:10), was important to him as a sign of his good faith and of the solidarity of his churches with the whole church.

In Jerusalem, however, his appearance in the temple provoked a riot because it was rumored that he smuggled a gentile into the holy place. Roman authorities intervened and took him into protective custody. Later he was transferred to Caesarea on the coast, where he remained in prison for more than two years. At last, he appealed to Caesar. The story is told in Acts 21:27—26:32.

For some reason, Acts devotes a whole chapter to the account of Paul's sea voyage to Italy (Acts 27) but tells almost nothing about what happened when he arrived in Rome. A delegation of Christians met him south of the city and accompanied him to the capitol. Apart from this detail, there is no further mention of the church in Rome. Paul was under house arrest for at least two years, but was free to preach and teach those who came to him (Acts 28:16, 30).

It has been suggested that the story in Acts ends here because Paul's trial had not yet come up, or because the book intended to present Paul favorably to the court when it did. Both suggestions are unlikely. It has also been argued that Paul was released and went to Spain as originally planned. This too is unlikely. What is probable is that he was among those executed in A.D. 64, by the Nero he had hoped would release him.

It has been thought that while he was in Rome Paul wrote the letters to Philippi, Colossae, Ephesus, and Philemon, and that after his release he wrote to Timothy twice and to Titus once. As already noted, it is more likely that the letters to Philippi, Colossae, and Philemon were written at Ephesus, and that Ephesians and the Pastoral Epistles (1, 2 Timothy, Titus) were written much later by one of his followers. If this is correct, then the last letter we have from Paul is the Epistle to the Romans.

The relation of Peter to Roman Christianity has been debated vigorously. Inevitably, the debate got mixed up with the whole issue of whether Peter was the first pope, and whether the church in Rome that bears his name actually stands on the place of his burial. The New Testament says nothing about Peter's being in Rome. However, Ignatius' letter to the Romans says that he does not "order" the Romans the way Peter and Paul did (Rom. 4). Not before the end of the second century do we get explicit statements about Peter's work in Rome, and many of these are clearly legendary. From the same era comes the tradition that there was a monument to Peter in Rome, though it is not clear whether it marked the place of burial or the place of martyrdom.

Every aspect of the topic "Peter in Rome" bristles with problems. Nonetheless, scholars generally agree that Peter did go to Rome, probably after Paul arrived. If his presence there had been known to Paul when he wrote the Epistle to the Romans, he would surely have mentioned him in the list of greetings in Romans 16 (unless, of course, Rom. 16 was not part of the original letter; some good manuscripts omit it). Later tradition speaks of the Roman church being founded by both Peter and Paul. This is not correct; rather, both apostles shaped early Christianity there for a brief period.

From the third century onward, tradition reports that both Peter and Paul were martyred in A.D. 64, in the persecution unleashed by Nero. Tradition also says Paul was beheaded, but that Peter was crucified—upside down upon his request, so that he would not die exactly like his Lord.

Nero's action against the Christians came upon the heels of the great fire. Neither the New Testament nor other Christian literature of the time mentions this fire. Our information comes primarily from the Roman historian, Tacitus, who wrote a generation later. According to Tacitus (Annals XV) the fire raged for six days, then broke out again, this time destroying more public buildings. Of fourteen districts, only four were unscathed, and three were leveled; the other half of the city was a shell. Gone were art treasures, ancient records, and the spoils of Roman conquests.

Tacitus reports two intriguing details. One, gangs prevented efforts to contain the fire, and some persons even spread the fire with torches, claiming that they were under orders. Tacitus suspects that they simply wanted their looting to go unhampered. Two, gossip linked Nero with the fire. Rumor spread that the emperor went to his private stage where he sang of the destruction of Troy (evidently the origin of the story that he "fiddled while Rome burned"). When the fire broke out the second time, people believed that he wanted to destroy the old city completely so he could rebuild it and name it after himself.

A generation after Tacitus, Seutonius states flatly that Nero set fire to the city and that he sang while it raged. Seutonius also says that Nero's agents looted the ruins for the emperor. How much of this is gossip and how much of it is true is difficult to decide. Still, these details reveal what people thought of their rulers!

Nero did, in fact, rebuild Rome. Broad straight streets replaced the old alleys. All buildings had to be partly of stone and each had to have its own walls. A better water supply was built, and all householders were required to keep fire fighting equipment on hand. Not surprisingly, some people complained that the new streets were hot, whereas the old narrow and twisted alleys had been shaded and cool!

To scotch the gossip about his role in the fire, Nero found a scapegoat—the Christians. Tacitus reports that Nero first had identifiable Christians arrested. Then, probably through torture, he learned the names of others. Although Tacitus despised the Christians, he reports that people pitied these innocent victims whose deaths were used to provide civic entertainment for Romans struggling to survive among the ashes. Christians were dressed in animal skins and then torn to pieces by dogs; others were crucified; some were set afire as torches in Nero's garden. Thus Nero became the first to use the power of the Roman government against the Christians.

The later saying, "The blood of the martyrs is the seed of the church" evidently was true also of this earliest persecution. Tacitus notes that these "notoriously depraved Christians (as they were popularly called) originated with Christ whom Pontius Pilate had executed." But he adds, "in spite of this temporary setback the deadly superstition had broken out afresh, not only in Judaea (where the mischief had started) but even in Rome. All degraded and shameful practices collect and flourish in the capital." (Quoted from Michael Grant, *The Jews in the Roman World,* p. 179.)

PAUL'S WORD TO THE FIRST GENERATION

Paul's Epistle to the Romans is the oldest document which can be linked with the church in the capital city. We have already noted Paul's stated reason for writing the letter. However, exactly how that reason—getting support for a mission to Spain—is related to the content of the letter is unclear. Why did his purpose lead him to put into writing the most complete exposition of the theology of justification by faith? Why must the readers go through more than fourteen chapters before they learn Paul's aim?

It is possible that Paul had an unstated aim in writing this letter—correcting misunderstanding. He may have known that he was being misrepresented in Rome, and may have wanted to share his theological understanding so that the Romans could deal with it directly, not by hearsay only. Paul clearly had some information about the church in Rome, because he addresses certain issues at the end of the letter. It is these chapters which will get our attention as we focus on two problems: the place of religious observances, and the attitude toward the government. The former is discussed in Romans 14—15, the latter in Romans 13:1-7.

Freedom of the Strong and Scruples of the Weak

Christians in Rome were divided over certain religious customs and observances. Circumcision was not a problem, apparently; nor does the cleavage seem to have been between Jewish and gentile Christians. Some were vegetarians, while others ate meat of various kinds. Some scrupulously observed holy days (including Sabbath? it is not mentioned specifically), whereas others treated all days alike. Paul's discussion does not suggest that the different viewpoints were part of the same theological issues which we saw in Galatia and Colossae, even though the same things—days and diets—were points of tension.

The issue, in other words, was not one of requirements for salvation, but of the basis on which the house churches could be one church. Paul detected a fundamental theological problem in these tensions nonetheless.

In Romans 15:1 Paul refers to "the strong" and in 14:1 to "the weak in faith." The "strong" are those who disregard the religious do's and don't's with respect to days and diets because, in the name of Christ, they eat what they wish to eat and ignore the days of special observances. These people call the scrupulous "weak in faith." The scrupulous would not have called themselves "weak in faith." They might have regarded themselves as the truly faithful, as those who take their religion seriously. Possibly "the strong" were also appealing to Paul, that is, to what they had heard about his theology.

Paul faced a delicate situation. He could hardly gain the support of Christians in Rome for his work in Spain if he were a controversial figure, if one group appealed to what they heard of him in order to argue with the other. As usual, there were people in the middle, unsure who was right. Under the circumstances, Paul might have tried to strengthen the hand of that group which stood closest to his own point of view. But that would have split the church wide open. Romans 14—15 show that Paul worked out a better alternative.

First, Paul makes it clear that he stands with "the strong" (notice the "we" in Rom. 15:1). He agrees that "everything is indeed clean"—that is, no food is forbidden (Rom. 14:20). This is consistent with his conviction that in Christ, one's relation to God is a matter of faith, not doing (both eating and abstaining are forms of "doing"). At the same time, Paul does not side with them in putting down those who disagree. It is the faith of "the strong" that should prevail, not "the strong" as a special group or party. That would be a victory for a particular group, but a defeat for the gospel.

In the second place, Paul's alternative involves several aspects, some addressed to all, some to one group or the other. To all Paul says, "let everyone be fully convinced in his own mind" (Rom. 14:5), whatever he does. Whether one observes days and dietary regulations or disregards them, one is to do it in honor of the Lord (Rom. 14:6-9). Paul grants that each does what he or she does as an act of faithfulness.

Therefore neither group is to despise the other. The person who eats anything must not look down on the one who abstains, and vice versa. After all, God welcomed both (Rom. 14:3-4). The terms of this welcome were thoroughly discussed in Rom. 1—12. In light of these considerations, they must welcome one another in their house churches and learn to live with each other's convictions.

Romans 14:10-12 would be specially appropriate for "the weak" —the brother or sister who, being careful to observe the rules, readily becomes judgmental. These people are "weak in faith" (Rom. 14:1) because they do not really believe that their relation to God depends entirely on trust. They are convinced that trust includes continued observance as a sign of obedience. Such persons easily condemn the non-observers for being lax or "worldly." But Paul asks them to stop being judges of other people's relation to God.

Interestingly, Paul's fullest counsel is addressed to those with whom he agrees—"the strong." They too are to cease expressing their superiority by passing out verdicts on the others (Rom. 14:13). Rather, precisely because they are strong, they should not cause "the weak" to stumble (Rom. 14:14, 21). Paul's meaning has often been twisted to mean, "If someone objects, don't do it." This is not what Paul means!

What Paul is getting at is far more profound, and calls for responsible use of freedom. The key is the word "stumble." The person who "stumbles" is not the one who simply takes offense, or who objects. Rather "stumbling" is doing something against one's conscience, eating or drinking without being "fully persuaded" that in Christ one is free to do so.

It is not difficult to imagine a situation which brings this out. Demetrius believes wholeheartedly that since his salvation depends solely on his faith, he is free to eat whatever he enjoys eating. But his fellow-Christian, Markus, disagrees and argues that if Demetrius were a real Christian he would not eat meat at all. Across the alley lives Gorgias, another Christian, who is not sure who is right; both Markus and Demetrius hound him, one to abstain, one to eat. One night, at Demetrius' house, a roast is served. Gorgias is in a bind. He does not want to offend his host, yet he is not really sure that being a Christian gives him freedom to eat any of it. Gorgias knows Markus will criticize him if he eats, and Demetrius will look down on him if he doesn't. But, being in Demetrius' house, he eats, though he doubts whether it is "all right."

From Paul's point of view, Demetrius has caused Gorgias to "stumble," to sin, for "whatever does not proceed from faith is sin" (Rom. 14:23)—the most radical definition of sin in the New Testament. To be sure, Gorgias does not sin because the meat is "unclean" or "off limits" in and of itself. Rather he sins because he suspects it might be "unclean" after all, and "it is unclean for anyone who thinks it is unclean" (Rom. 14:14).

Doubtless Demetrius is pleased that he has gotten Gorgias to eat, that Gorgias is now "liberated" too. Yet Paul says that Demetrius should not try to please himself. Rather he should do whatever is best for Gorgias, just as Christ did not do whatever was pleasing to himself but what was good for the neighbor (Rom. 15:1-3). So if the weak and inwardly uncertain brother or sister is induced to violate conscience, the strong, free brother is not living on the basis of love (Rom. 14:15).

In any case, God's kingdom is not a matter of food and drink. As Paul had written the Corinthians, "Food will not commend us to God; we are no worse off if we do not eat and no better off if we do" (1 Cor. 8:8). Unfortunately, many Christians have never believed Paul at this point.

It might appear that Paul is asking the free, "strong" Christian to forego Christ-given freedom, to forfeit freedom for the sake of this brother or sister who is not yet as free, and might never be. But this would misunderstand Paul. Actually, Paul implies that the Christian is truly free in Christ when one is free to stop insisting that others be free in exactly the same way as oneself, when one is free to forego making "a big thing" out of this freedom. The truly free Christian is not compulsive about showing off this freedom, especially to the detriment of the hesitant. Rather, Christian freedom includes freedom to forego exercising this freedom whenever it jeopardizes the brother or sister. Precisely because "the strong" knows that he or she is free, the greater responsibility rests on him or her (1 Cor. 8:7-13).

Christian freedom, as Paul understands it, does not homogenize persons into a church of the like-minded. Instead, it makes space where honest differences can be maintained in love. Paul envisioned what we call a "pluralistic" church long before it became fashionable today. It would be a mistake to infer that Paul was asking that there be no more discussion of the matter, that each "do his own thing." What should cease is the constant hectoring of one another.

Once the Roman Christians begin to be concerned for one another and not simply for maintaining their own point of view, they will be on the way to "testing out" what the will of God is for them (Rom. 12:1-3). That is what Christian pluralism is all about.

Rome as God's Servant

One may wish that Paul had never brought up the subject of obedience to government. What he said in Romans 13:1-7 has been used repeatedly by tyrants and government-appointed churchmen alike to keep Christians in line. Verse 4 has also been used to argue the case for capital punishment.

A few scholars have suggested that Paul himself did not actually write this notorious paragraph, and that someone added it later (though very early, since all manuscripts have it). Indeed, no specifically Christian reason is given for this total submission to civil authority. Moreover, it seems inconsistent with 1 Corinthians 6:1-6, where Paul urges Christians not to take their law suits against each other to the civil courts—implying that they should not grant the courts jurisdiction over themselves. Paul may, of course, have changed his mind before writing to the Romans, or simply have been inconsistent. In any case, arguments on behalf of the view that Paul did not write this passage have not persuaded most students.

Paul, of course, cannot be blamed for what was made of his words later. But he can be held accountable for what he said in his own time. After all, he calls for unqualified submission to all government authorities because they wield God-given authority. Whoever opposes them opposes what God instituted. He goes on to say that those who do what is right will have no reason to fear the police, and urges the readers to pay all taxes and render whatever honor is due the authorities.

It is hard to imagine anyone writing more of a blank check. It never seems to cross Paul's mind that there might be situations in which submission and obedience ought to be withheld. The long history of Christian civil disobedience dissents from Paul here. Paul appears to allow for no exceptions.

Paul does not speak for the whole New Testament. Jesus, it will be recalled (see chap. 2), separated obedience to God from obedience to Caesar. John, the author of the Book of Revelation, forced a choice between obedience to God and obedience to Caesar, whom he viewed as the instrument of Satan. But Paul presents a third view—that Caesar is the agent of God. What Jesus distinguishes and the Book of Revelation opposes, Paul combines.

It is not clear just why Paul writes this way. There are three kinds of explanations. One explanation is that Paul was writing early in Nero's reign, when people were still optimistic about its potential. Accordingly, it has been suggested that Paul would have written differently had he foreseen Nero's persecution. Paul may have been favorably disposed toward the empire, but this does not explain the passage, and neither does the optimism of the time. The last paragraph of the chapter (Rom. 13:11-14) points to something else—belief that the End is near.

Another explanation is that what elicited this passage was not Paul's view of government, but his view of Christian salvation. Paul is dealing with a tendency, assumed to be present in Rome no less than in his own churches, to regard with contempt the institutions and laws of this world because Christians are "free from the law" altogether. Christians who were influenced by gnostic ideas advocated a kind of Christian anarchism as a sign of their complete liberation from this world. The trouble with this explanation, however, is that the reasons given for unhesitating submission have nothing whatever to do with such a view of salvation.

A third possibility is that Paul asserts that government is ordained by God because he suspected that some were saying the opposite—that the government and its agents were instruments of Satan.

It is more likely that Paul brought up the subject in the first place, and then treated it as he did, because he surmised that these points needed to be made. Less than ten years before, Claudius had expelled Jews from the city, including Jewish Christians. By this time, many had returned. Perhaps he wanted to avoid giving Nero any excuse to repeat the precedent. Paul may have known how precarious was the legal status of the Christian house churches in Rome, and may have wanted to head off any harassment. (The "every person" in v. 1 means every Christian, not every inhabitant of the empire; Paul's letters never address the public at large.)

Whatever may have motivated Paul, the fact is that the passage doubtless created more problems for Christians than it ever solved. Paul himself was a victim of Nero's brutal, and perhaps illegal, persecution. Moreover, the innocent Christians whom Nero tortured discovered that Romans 13:3-4 is wrong: rulers are a terror not only to the wicked but also to those who do good. Tragically, the innocent victims of governmental persecution have had to ratify that discovery with their blood—down to our own time.

Still, it is important to see what Paul said and did not say, and to see both in relation to his time. First, the paragraph does not intend to present a full-blown outline of Paul's view of government, and even less a "doctrine of the state." (Unfortunately, the Jerusalem Bible translates verse 4 as "the state is there to serve God for your benefit;" there is no word for "state" in the text.) The whole passage concerns Christian conduct with respect to governing power in a situation where the only options are obedience or prosecution. Paul counsels Christians who live under a government whose power is absolute and whose structure cannot be changed. Indeed, the house churches could not challenge it at all.

Second, as already noted, there is nothing specifically Christian in Romans 13:1-7. It was common to regard the empire as God's gift to humanity for the common good. Furthermore, Paul's statements are rather restrained in comparison with what others had been saying about the empire. Moreover, it is not clear that Paul speaks of the emperor at all, as the RSV suggests in verse 3; it translates "he who is in authority" and in verse 4 goes on to speak of "he." The text actually has simply "authority," and seems to have in view the government authorities whom the Christians would be dealing with, not the emperor.

In any case, Paul does not write what emperors would have preferred him to write—that the emperor embodies a divine genius or power. Likewise, when Paul asks that honor be given to whomever honor is due, he does not say that this includes divine honors.

Finally, throughout the passage Paul quietly sets government authority under the authority of God. There is no blurring of lines between political power and divine power. The real power to be respected ultimately is God's. Government has God-given responsibility for the good (v. 4; literally, "God's servant for you for the good"). Because Paul here writes always of God and never of Christ, one must reject the suggestion that Paul thinks Christ's resurrection put government rulers (the agents of the heavenly powers) under his authority, so that now government operates (unwittingly) as Christ's agent.

The more one views this paragraph in light of the times, the more likely it is that Paul was seeking a way to give judicious counsel to Roman Christians. They were to be obedient subjects in good conscience without being caught up in the glorification of the empire, on the one hand, and without repudiating it wholesale as devilish, on the other. It is unfortunate that what originally was intended to suggest a limit to imperial power (set by God as a servant for good) was later taken as justification for tyranny —"the divine right of kings."

ISSUES FACING THE SECOND GENERATION

The setting of second generation Christianity in Rome is the reign of Domitian (A.D. 81-96). The Roman church is reflected in the letter which the church sent to Corinth at the end of Domitian's reign. The letter is known as the First Epistle of Clement to distinguish it from another document written later by someone else, the so-called Second Letter of Clement.

Another writing also shows us some aspects of Christianity in Rome because it was sent to the Roman church—the Epistle to the Hebrews. This book must have been fairly popular in Rome, for Clement uses it several times. Since Hebrews 12:4 says the readers have not yet faced martyrdom, Hebrews was probably written early in Domitian's reign (about A.D. 85-90). We shall look briefly at each of these.

Tired Christians

The problems that go with sagging faith and second thoughts are addressed in the book sometimes called "The Epistle of Paul to the Hebrews." However, it is not an epistle (letter) but a theological essay motivated by strong pastoral concern; the concluding personal touches (Heb. 13:23-24) give it only the appearance of a letter. It was not written to Hebrews (Jews), but to Christians. An early copiest gave it the present title because he thought that the intricate discussion of the Old Testament was intended to interest "Hebrews." Nor is Paul the author, although it got into the New Testament mainly because the church in Egypt continued to think it was from Paul.

The book itself is anonymous. In the third century, even Egypt's leading theologian, Origen, had to conclude that only God knows who wrote it. None of the suggestions which have been made since then are really better. Hebrews 13:24 suggests that the writer is among Italians who send greetings to the readers (presumably in Rome) the way Tennesseans in Dallas might send greetings with a letter to a church in Nashville.

Hebrews is usually studied for its theology, written in the best Greek in the New Testament. Here, however, we are interested chiefly in the readers because it was their problems that called forth this theological treatise. Four aspects of their situation give us a rough profile of Roman Christianity in A.D. 85. Here too we must not confuse the author's understanding of the readers with their understanding of themselves. An opinion poll probably would yield a quite different self-image among the readers. That likelihood, of course, is precisely what prompted someone to write what he did.

First, in Hebrews 2:1 the writer senses a danger—the readers might "drift away" from the gospel. It is sometimes said that they were about to slip back into Judaism, but this was hardly the case. The danger, rather, was giving up, not persevering in their faithfulness (Heb. 3:6, 14). "Back-sliding" has serious consequences, the writer points out. The generation of the Israelites who left Egypt were faithless in the wilderness; consequently they did not enter the promised land (here called "rest," Heb. 3:15-19). The same thing can happen again—this time to Christians (Heb. 4). In fact, whoever abandons the gospel cannot return, or repent a second time (Heb. 6:4-8; see also 10:26-31; 12:15-17).

This is indeed a "hard saying." Hebrews is the first to face the question of repentance after repudiation of Christianity—an issue which became very divisive in North Africa after the third century persecutions.

It is useful to reflect on other New Testament texts. Matthew, we recall, included Jesus' warning that on Judgment Day it would take more than confessing Jesus as Lord to gain admission into the Kingdom (Matt. 7:21). John's Gospel too cautions Christians that unless they adhere closely to Jesus and "bear fruit" God will prune them away (John 15:1-11). The Book of Revelation threatens the churches of Asia Minor that if they do not repent they will be destroyed (e.g., Ephesus will have its lamp removed; Rev. 2:5).

It is not accidental that such warnings are found in the literature of the second generation, for whom the gospel has become routine. In contrast with the first generation Christians in Corinth who claimed too much for their salvation, the second generation began to take it for granted. One after another, writers in the second generation deal with this problem, each in his own way.

Second, Hebrews 5:11—6:2 reveals a different problem— stunted growth in understanding the Christian faith. Those who should have developed to the point where they could be teachers still need to learn the ABC's. Nonetheless, the writer is not going to teach them the elemental things again (Heb. 6:1). Instead, he wants to pull them toward the deeper, more advanced, meaning of Christian faith and life. He will do this from chapter 7 onward. The writer denies the possibility of a second repentance in the same breath in which he criticizes the readers for being immature. Evidently he fears that if they will not keep on growing they will fall away and forfeit their salvation altogether.

The theological argument in this book is not easy to follow— it was not supposed to be! It was intended to pull the readers into deeper waters. Furthermore, the writer is persuaded that understanding the deeper meanings of Christianity better will help the readers become more faithful Christians. For him, understanding and doing go together. Repeatedly, he states the "practical consequences" of the theology which he presents. He believes that complacent Christians can be aroused by theological understanding. To what extent was he naive? To what extent was he right?

What the author considers the ABC's also gives us a glimpse into Christianity of the time. There are six items in the list (Heb. 6:1-2), and they fall naturally into three pairs: repentance and faith, baptisms (RSV: ablutions) and laying on of hands (giving the Holy Spirit to the newly baptized), and resurrection and eternal judgment. The first pair has to do with requirements for entrance into the church, the second with rituals of entry, and the last with future salvation.

Not a word is said here about Christ. This should not mislead us, however, for Christ is evidently implied in "faith toward God." Likewise, the fact that the Lord's Supper is ignored does not mean that it was unimportant. Rather, it did not belong to the decisive elements in the process of becoming a Christian or attaining salvation.

The "instruction about baptisms" probably does not mean that Christians were practicing repeated washings and baptisms, but that they were instructed about the meaning of Christian baptism in contrast with baptism and ritual washings being practiced by other religions. In other words, the church was careful to provide a precise understanding of what baptism did and did not mean. Unfortunately for us, the writer did not reveal what he believed it meant; after all, he said he was not going to repeat the ABC's.

Third, according to Hebrews 10:23-25, some are neglecting Christian worship. Perhaps they no longer took it seriously (Heb. 12:25-29). It is also possible that this neglect was part of the disappointment over the fact that the Lord had not come. Early Christians nurtured the expectation of the Lord's coming, especially at worship.

We see this in the prayer, "Our Lord come" (1 Cor. 16:22). This was originally spoken in Aramaic *(Maran atha!)*; evidently Paul taught it in Aramaic to the Corinthians, because he assumes they will understand it when he spells it in Greek without translating it. Moreover, in 1 Corinthians 11:26, where Paul comments on the Supper (the heart of early Christian worship), he says that every time they eat the bread and drink the cup they "proclaim the Lord's death until he comes." Interestingly, the same *Maran atha* prayer occurs in the Didache (pronounced Did-a-kay'), a Christian writing from the end of the first century or later.

In other words, Christian worship celebrated the expected Coming. If Christians were disappointed because this had not occurred, one can understand why some would neglect worship. One can also understand why the writer would describe the readers as having "drooping hands" and "weak knees" (Heb. 12:12). Their faith is sagging.

We can also understand other emphases. The roster of the heroes of faith (Heb. 11) reaches its climax in the point that none of them "received what was promised," but they persevered nonetheless. Christians too should "run with patience the race" set before them while their predecessors are looking on (Heb. 12:1). For this writer, salvation is real but not yet visible. We do not yet see that Jesus is Lord over all, but what we can "see" is the lowly and suffering Jesus (Heb. 2:5-9). The whole point of explaining Christ's heavenly priesthood (which is invisible from earth) is to help the readers understand that what is confessed is real and permanent precisely because it is not visible now. If it were, it would belong to this world, which is not permanent.

Hebrews gives a unique definition of faith as the "assurance of things hoped for, the conviction [of the reality] of things not seen" (Heb. 11:1). For this writer, "the really real" is permanent and invisible, while what is visible is transient. If someone had objected, "But I don't *see* any salvation," the author would have replied, "Of course you don't. That's why it's real." For many persons today, by contrast, what is "really real" is visible, measurable, and touchable while what is invisible is unreal.

Fourth, Hebrews 10:32-34 and 12:4 indicate that Christians have suffered public abuse. Even though they have not been killed, some have been in prison, and have had their property confiscated. Yet they remained steadfast; those who were left alone did not avoid associating with the harassed but identified with them (see also 6:10). Yet, evidently, the writer is not sure they will "keep on keeping on," especially if they doubt that their salvation is real. So he reminds them that formerly they established a good track record because they knew they had a better, permanent "possession" with God than any they might have had in Rome. He also interprets the hardship they must endure as God's discipline for their ultimate good (Heb. 12:5-11).

It is strange that the writer says the readers have not yet had to deal with martyrdom. Has he forgotten Nero's persecution? This is unlikely. Another explanation is possible. Tacitus' account of Nero's persecution implies that Christianity was virtually stamped out, but that it "broke out" again.

In other words, the Christians in Rome at the end of the century might not have experienced Nero's persecution themselves and they may not have been descendants of those who did. The Christians to whom Hebrews was written could have constituted a church which began afresh after Nero's time, even if its nucleus might have gone back to the earliest days. This "second" church in Rome would not have had to deal with martyrdom—yet.

Hebrews is a strange book for most readers today, almost as difficult to read with understanding as the Book of Revelation. Readers are easily lost in the complicated explanation of Christ's high priesthood and few get excited over Melchizedek (Heb. 7). However, if one approaches this book for what it is—a theologian's word to a church grown complacent—then it may dawn on us that Hebrews was written for the kind of Christianity which many people today know best. We can scarcely read this book without asking, What sort of theological exposition of the Christian faith might do for our time what Hebrews was intended to do in its time?

Unpredictable Terror

Another reign of terror came during the latter years of Domitian's reign. There was no systematic effort to stamp out Christianity; instead, individual Christians faced arbitrary arrests and punishments. Although later Christians portrayed Domitian as another Nero, Roman historians do not report that he persecuted Christians. Still, there is no reason to doubt the Christians' memory, even if they magnified experiences which Roman historians would not have thought important enough to record.

Domitian's reign was marked also by solid achievement, at least at first. He was the son of Vespasian, who had commanded the forces sent by Nero to quell the Jewish revolt in A.D. 66. His older brother, Titus, had captured the city after Vespasian returned to become emperor. When Vespasian died, Titus succeeded him for two years. Titus' death meant that at last, it was Domitian's turn.

At first things began well enough. Seutonius reports that Domitian restored many buildings which had been ruined by another fire in A.D. 80. He restocked libraries even though he had no great interest in learning. He prohibited human castration, evidently in order to check the rising demand for eunuch slaves, whose price he now controlled strictly. He undertook to reform the courts, and ruled that if any juryman had taken bribes the whole jury would be penalized. He encouraged people to bring charges against officials suspected of corruption, and punished police informers who, by making false charges, got estates confiscated (and doubtless lined their pockets).

Domitian rigorously collected the tax on the Jews which his father had required them to pay after the fall of Jerusalem. Previously this money had been collected by the Jews themselves and sent to the temple. After A.D. 70, the money went to the emperor. Now, it seems, he discovered tax evasion: according to Seutonius, some Jews kept their identity secret and some gentiles practiced Judaism but never became circumcised proselytes. Both were required to pay the tax.

Seutonius reports that enforcement was relentless. One day when he was in court he saw a ninety year old man stripped to see whether he had been circumcised. Yet we hear of no systematic harassment of tax-paying, law-abiding Jews; evidently the legal status of the synagogues was not jeopardized.

In persecuting individuals Domitian did not spare his cousin, Titus Flavius Clemens and his wife Domitilla: he was executed, and his wife and daughter were exiled. A later historian says they were accused of "atheism," a charge brought against those who

150

accepted Jewish customs, and later a standard accusation against Christians because they denied the gods. We recall that Domitian insisted on being called "Lord and God" or "Lord God." Whether this family had converted to Judaism or Christianity is unclear. Some scholars believe that T. Flavius Clemens was friendly to Christians, and that Domitilla might have been a Christian. If they are correct, Christianity had reached the highest levels of society.

Domitian's cruel streak now came to the fore. He ordered unusual tortures and arbitrary executions. The property of the victims was confiscated, partly to pay for building projects (including an artificial lake for mock naval battles), and partly to pay for a raise in pay for the troops. Seutonius reports that he was everywhere feared and hated, except in the army. Finally he was murdered.

Christianity Institutionalized

Clement began his letter to the Corinthians by apologizing for not writing sooner "because of a series of misfortunes" which suddenly came upon the church. Possibly this was an allusion to the problems created by arbitrary arrests and persecutions by Domitian's police. The Corinthian church was split by dissension, and the Roman church tried to heal the situation. A delegation of long-time Christians was sent to Corinth, doubtless carrying Clement's letter with them (1 Clem. 63:3; 65:1).

One has the impression that Clement writes so passionately about jealously and strife because he has had to deal with these also at home. For him, order, peace, and harmony are fundamental. Clement is the voice of institutionalized Christianity in Rome at the end of the century.

Clement writes from the standpoint of a bishop who regards dissent as a challenge to properly established leadership. He argues that God sent Jesus, Jesus sent the apostoles, and the apostles appointed bishops and deacons (1 Clem. 42:2-4) because they knew "there would be strife over the title of bishop" (1 Clem. 44:1). Clement provides important evidence for the developing office of bishop. However, he does not yet sharply distinguish bishops from presbyters (elders), for he uses the terms interchangeably.

What matters is that there be revolt against the leadership: "Surely we will be guilty of no small sin if we thrust out of office of bishop" those who have served well. "You will not find that upright men have ever been thrust out by holy men" (1

151

Clem. 44:4; 45:3). In other words, those who are disgruntled are rascals (see also 54; 57:1; also Heb. 13:7 urges that readers respect and imitate the leadership). It is possible that the dissidents had reason to be unhappy with the bishop; in Clement's mind, that is of secondary importance.

Perhaps Clement's own passion to keep a low profile so as not to provoke the police irritated some of the brothers and sisters. Clement does not charge the dissidents with theological errors, but with insubordination. What he says about government authority could easily make some persons unhappy. He finds the model of Christian orderly obedience in the army because there each person stays in his place and carries out the orders of the emperor (1 Clem. 37:1-3). One does not find the ideal in something one despises or regards as Satanic.

Moreover, Clement includes a prayer (chaps. 59-61) in which he not only prays for the government, whose power is given by God, but asks God's help in being subject to it, "in no way resisting thy will." With this, Clement clearly stands in the line of Romans 13, and nothing the state has done, not even Domitian's insistence on being called "Lord and God," has caused him to respond as did John on Patmos.

Since the prayer was probably taken from the liturgy of the church, it represents the stance of the church as a whole. Moreover, the liturgy was in the hands of the leadership. Consequently anyone who objected to what it said about the emperor in fact challenged the church's leaders. In any case, it was Clement and the leadership who prevailed, not the dissidents.

Second, Clement's letter is important because it shows that the church at Rome assumed that it had a right to intervene in the Corinthian situation. Although Clement takes this right for granted, he does not suggest that he is writing to subordinates. Rather he assumes that a letter from Rome will not be resented but listened to, and that the delegation will be well received. To undergird the authority of the letter, Clement claims what no New Testament writing except the Revelation to John claims—that it was written "through the Holy Spirit" (1 Clem. 63:2; 2 Tim. 3:16 talks about the Old Testament). In other words, with 1 Clement we begin to see the Roman church emerge as a leader of churches—a development which eventually led to the papacy.

Third, Clement's letter shows that there was disillusionment because the Lord had not come as expected, as well as doubt about the future resurrection of Christians. Clement quotes a "Scripture" passage which he hopes will not apply to Corinthians and Romans: "Wretched are the double minded, those who harbor doubts in their souls and say, 'We have heard these things even in our father's time and yet here we are, already grown old, and none of these things has happened to us' " (1 Clem. 23:3). This sounds like the quotation in 2 Peter 3:4. We do not know what "Scripture" Clement is quoting. The Second Letter of Clement also uses this lost writing and calls it "a prophetic word"—that is, an apocalypse. Evidently it was used so frequently that Clement can quote it as if it were part of the Bible.

Interestingly, Clement does not really deal with the disappointment except to say that the Coming will surely occur, just as fruit appears on grape vines in due course. Later, he says that the Lord will indeed come to reward each person for his deeds (1 Clem. 34:3). Curiously, to undergrid the Christian hope of resurrection he appeals to the tall tale about the phoenix, a bird said to live 500 years, and from whose body there emerges a worm which grows wings and after 500 years returns! One wonders what is happening to Christian theology when belief in resurrection is supposed to be strengthened by an oddity in the zoo—even if such a bird existed.

Fourth, Clement's letter reveals the extent to which the Roman church has taken into its way of understanding Christianity the general moral teachings of the day. For example, when Clement urges Christians to maintain peace and order because this is what creation reveals (1 Clem. 19, 20, 33), he simply echoes the Stoic way of thinking. The few references to Jesus regard him as a teacher of moral truths. His death is spoken of only in passing, not as a theme with theological power.

Throughout, Clement emphasizes that the moral character of Christians will be rewarded in this life by peace and stability, and in the next life as well. What Hebrews insisted upon—that Christians are strangers and pilgrims who have no abiding city here on earth (Heb. 13:13-14)—Clement simply ignores. Instead, he represents a trend—Christians, no longer eagerly expecting the Lord, are settling down in the world. For Paul, "salvation is nearer to us now than when we first believed" (Rom. 13:11). For Clement and the trend he represents, it was not much nearer even though thirty years had passed.

Fifth, Clement shows the way many Christians were reading the Bible (the Greek translation of the Old Testament). For Clement, as for the synagogues, the Bible is primarily a history of righteous and devout persons who are to be imitated. There is no real interest in the history of Israel as the story of God's election and purpose. The fact that he appears to quote from memory shows that he is thoroughly at home in the Greek Bible. Evidently it presented him with no theological difficulties in interpretation.

Finally, the way Clement used early Christian writings shows an important stage in the development of the New Testament alongside the synagogue's Bible. It is difficult to tell whether Clement used any of our gospels because, in the first place, Matthew, Luke, and John were probably written about the same time as Clement, but not in Rome. Even if Clement had read these Gospels, they would have been so new that they would not yet be authorities to be quoted in a letter to Corinth. He may have used Mark, probably written in Rome twenty-five or thirty years earlier, but this is far from clear. He appears rather to have used some of the same materials which the Evangelists used.

We must bear in mind that Jesus' sayings and stories about him were still circulating by word of mouth. No written account was as important to Christians then as it has come to be for us, nor as fixed. Teachers could combine them in various ways as needed. We can see this freedom in 1 Clement 13:1-2:

Above all, remember the words of the Lord Jesus which he uttered while teaching forebearance and patience. "Be merciful that you may receive mercy. Forgive that forgiveness may be given to you; as you do, so shall it be done to you; as you judge, so shall you be judged; as you show kindness, so will kindness be showed to you; the measure you give will be the measure you get."

We recognize these sayings from the Sermon on the Mount (Matt. 5-7) and the Sermon on the Plain (Luke 6); yet what Clement gives is not a precise quotation of either Matthew or Luke. Clement's freedom to compile and paraphrase is typical of the time.

Clement apparently knew several of Paul's letters: Romans, 1 Corinthians, Galatians, and Philippians. Curiously, he does not seem to have known 2 Corinthians, the two letters to the Thessalonians, Ephesians, Colossians or the Pastorals (1, 2 Timothy, Titus). The Pastorals, of course, were probably written later than Clement's time, and there is no reason why he should have used Philemon. Clement is too far removed from apocalyptic thought to have relied on 2 Thessolanians, but it is strange that he did not use 2 Corinthians and 1 Thessalonians because at certain points he deals with topics discussed also in these epistles. On the other hand, Clement clearly used Hebrews.

These writings are not yet regarded as Scripture, as authoritative writings alongside the Old Testament. Yet, the influence of this literature on Clement, and on the Roman Church, is manifest. We are on the way to the development of a New Testament, but not yet there.

It is useful to summarize what Clement's letter shows us about the Roman church at the end of the first century. There had been a challenge to the leadership, but it was not successful. The office of bishop was growing stronger. The expectation of the Lord's coming was no longer a center which affected all other considerations (as had been the case with Paul) but had become one of the things Christians still were supposed to believe, despite doubts about it. Despite Domitian's terror, the church refused to criticize the empire; to the contrary, it was eager to live in peace.

Moreover, relations with the synagogues must have been reasonably good, because there is no hint of tensions like those found in Matthew and John. In fact, the religious and moral teachings which had developed in the Hellenistic synagogues were being used freely by Roman Christians also. The Old Testament was taken for granted as the Scripture, and interpreting it appeared to present no fundamental theological questions. There is no hint in Rome of what the so-called Letter of Barnabas will say shortly in Egypt—that the Old Testament never did belong to the Jews but belonged to Christians from the start.

Finally, the church had developed into a stable institution and did not hesitate to assert itself as a leader. Before another century passed, it would appeal to the work of Peter and Paul to undergird its emerging role in Christianity.

THE THIRD GENERATION AND BEYOND

In the second century, Roman Christianity thrived. During the decade of A.D. 140-150 Rome was the most exciting and diversified center of Christianity we know of. Describing these developments, even with modest detail, would take us too far afield. We will, however, take account of persecution, schism, and heresy in order to round out the picture and point to the future.

Persecution Guidelines

Domitian was succeeded by Nerva, an old man who died after reigning from A.D. 96-98. He undid much of Domitian's "cult of personality" much as Krushchev de-Stalinized the Soviet Union. Nerva was followed by two emperors who strengthened the empire, Trajan (A.D. 98-117) and Hadrian (A.D. 117-138). Both encouraged emperor worship and persecuted Christians, though with some restraint. In A.D. 113 Trajan found it necessary to provide administrative guidelines for the persecution in northern Asia Minor.

It was in Trajan's time that Ignatius arrived in Rome to be executed. At the end of Hadrian's reign, the bishop of Rome, Telesphoros, was executed. What led up to this we do not know.

The persecution of Asia Minor Christians is of special importance because Trajan's representative, Pliny, exchanged letters with the emperor on the subject. Pliny knows that Christianity must be suppressed, because it has become far too influential. Men and women of all ages and of every class have caught this superstition, even in the countryside. Temples have been neglected, but thanks to his procedures, people are returning to them. Once again people are buying meat which had been sacrificed to the gods. As a result of his repressive acts, both religion and the economy are picking up again.

Still, Pliny has some questions. Exactly what is the crime—is it simply being Christian or is it what Christians do and do not do? Should punishment take account of differences in age and sex? Should those who renounce Christianity be pardoned? To help Trajan understand the situation, Pliny reports the procedures he has been using.

First, when persons alleged to be Christians are brought before him, Pliny asks whether they are guilty or not. If they admit it, he repeats the question twice and points out the consequences. When they persist, he orders those who have Roman citizenship sent to Rome for punishment, and executes the rest. Apparently Christians had many enemies, because Pliny says that as the investigations proceed, the accusations become more numerous. Indeed, he even received an unsigned list accusing many person of being Christians.

Second, for those who denied the charge of being Christian, Pliny devised his own form of a lie-detector test. He brought in a statue of the emperor and order the accused to call upon the gods, to worship the emperor with wine and incense, and to curse Christ —because he has heard that real Christians cannot be forced to do these things. But some did as he commanded, though they admitted that they had once been Christians, sometimes as long as twenty years before (that is, they had abandoned Christianity during Domitian's persecution).

Third, Pliny used these ex-Christians to learn what Christianity was all about. They told him that once a week (presumably on Sunday) they met before sunrise and recited a hymn to Christ as to a god, took an oath not to rob, commit adultery, break their word, or defraud. Then they adjourned to have a common meal. Pliny checked this report by torturing two slave deaconesses.

In this reply, Trajan agreed that Christians are to be punished, but the police are not to take the initiative in finding them. Anonymous accusations are to be rejected (otherwise, the government would be returning to the policies of Domitian). Anyone who denies being a Christian and proves this by worshipping the Roman gods, is to be pardoned, regardless of his previous allegiance to Christianity. Clearly, Trajan is trying to suppress Christianity without unleashing a witch-hunt. It is clear, moreover, that simply being a Christian was a crime, even though it is not clear precisely why it was.

We have discussed this correspondence in some detail because it casts light on the third generation in Asia Minor, and also provides the setting for a third generation book which was written from Rome to the Christians there—1 Peter. (Even those who think this letter comes from the early 60's do not maintain that Peter himself dictated it because it uses excellent Greek. So Peter is said to have told Silvanus more or less what to write.) First Peter reflects precisely the situation in A.D. 113—people suffer because they are "Christians" (1 Pet. 4:16).

First Peter 3:15 urges the readers, "Always be prepared to make a defense to anyone who calls you to account for the hope that is in you, yet do it with gentleness and reverence." This fits well with the Christians' situation in Pliny's court. The author goes on to say that if they must suffer, they should make sure that they are innocent (1 Pet. 3:3-17; 4:15), and appeals to the example of Christ.

Nonetheless, Christians in Asia Minor are urged not to resist Roman power. Rather, 1 Peter 2:13-14 urges them to "be subject for the Lord's sake to every human institution, whether it be to the emperor as supreme, or to governors as sent by him to punish those who do wrong and to praise those who do right" (a clear echo of Rom. 13:1-7). Doubtless this was the policy also in Rome, even if it is "Babylon"—the word used of the city in Revelation 17 (1 Pet. 5:13).

Schism

In July, 144, the Roman church expelled Marcion (we noted the main points of his teaching in chap. 1). He was as determined as he was convinced he was right, and so started his own church. The movement spread rapidly, and endured for several centuries as a rival church.

The Roman church did not put up long with Marcion, for he had arrived there in about A.D. 140. He came from Smyrna, where Polycarp had rebuffed him as "the first born of Satan."

Before that, he had been expelled from the church in Pontus (northern Asia Minor) by the bishop, who was also his father. It was said later that he had violated "a virgin"—probably the church rather than a girl, for it was common to regard the church as a pure virgin until heretics came along.

When Marcion arrived in Rome he became a member of the church and is reported to have given it a sizeable sum of money as well. In a few years, however, his views could no longer be tolerated, and he was expelled. Now the main-line congregations had a rival church to contend with.

Marcionite congregations, as we saw, were provided with a purely Christian Bible: the letters of Paul and the Gospel of Luke, all of which Marcion edited by removing passages favorable to the Old Testament, the Creator, and the Creator's world. He did not think that Paul and Luke had been wrong, of course. Rather, he was convinced that their writings had been corrupted later by Christians who did not see how radical Christian salvation really was. Marcion was the first person who undertook to restore original Christianity; he saw himself as a reformer. The church at Rome, however, saw him as a heretic.

Marcion's congregations must have been hard to distinguish from the church catholic, at least in some respects. They retained the sacraments, although they used only bread and water in the Eucharist (as did some other groups of the time). They used the Lord's Prayer also, but changed it to say, "Give us this day your bread." This change made the petition request the eucharist bread, not the daily bread which comes from the Creator's world. The Marcionite churches also were organized more or less like the main church.

The growing sacramentalism of the Roman church is shown by the fact that it accepted Marcionite baptism as valid. Evidently the same rite and formula were used in both types of Christianity. Later, however, it was reported that the Marcionites baptized only those who had renounced sexual relations. Sexuality, after all, was part of the Creator's evil world and must be renounced as part of one's salvation. In the third century, the Roman church had to debate whether Marcionite baptism was acceptable after all.

Heresy and Orthodoxy

About the same time that Marcion arrived in Rome, three other figures appeared as well. One was Justin, a well-to-do philosopher from Samaria. After he became a Christian in Ephesus, he came to Rome where he set up a school to teach and defend Christianity as the full truth of which philosophy had only bits and pieces and of which the Old Testament had spoken as well. He was martyred in A.D. 150.

The second figure was one of Justin's pupils, Tatian, a Syrian with an excellent Greek education. Tatian however came to think that Christianity should not be so open to philosophy as Justin implied. He broke with the church at Rome, and returned to Syria where he started his own type of Christianity noted for its asceticism. He is remembered chiefly for the fact that he wove together the four Gospels into one narrative. This became the only form of the gospel story used in Syrian churches for the next three hundred years. Of his other writings, only a few survived, as is true in Justin's case also.

Justin and Marcion probably agreed on almost nothing, except that Jesus is the Savior. Justin is said to have debated the philosopher Crescens, whom later Christians accused of instigating Justin's execution. Be that as it may, it would have been even more fascinating to hear Justin and Marcion debate—if in fact they did.

The third famous theologian who was in Rome at the same time was Valentinus, the most influential gnostic teacher of the time. He almost became bishop of Rome. Valentinus, some think, may have written some of the books found in the gnostic library which was discovered in Egypt in 1947. Valentinianism itself developed into a diverse movement; its greatest impact, however, was in Egypt. Still, one wonders what might have happened if Valentinus had become bishop in Rome!

It must have been exciting to be a Christian in Rome in the time when Marcion, Justin, Tatian, and Valentinus were advocating quite diverse theologies. Of these, only Justin stood in what would become the mainstream. In the others the church detected serious dangers which had to be dealt with.

The defense of the church against teachings which it regarded as dangerous or plainly perverse was threefold, as we have already seen: canon, creed, clergy (chap. 3). In Rome, the development of all three can be traced more clearly than elsewhere. The role of the bishop began to be strengthened already in Clement's day. The creed, of course, was the baptismal confession which has come to be called "The Apostles Creed"; its long development cannot be traced here. Our interest lies rather in the canon—the emergence of the New Testament.

At the end of the second century, someone in Rome drew up a list of books which the church accepted as suitable for use in worship and teaching. It is called the Muratorian Canon because

159

a man named Muratori found it in 1740. The Muratorian Canon shows how much closer to the New Testament we are at the end of the second century than we were in Clement's day.

The list shows that the church in Rome accepted only our four Gospels (and used them in the same order as we do). It also accepted the Book of Acts, letters from Paul to seven churches (said to represent the whole church as do the seven letters in Rev. 2—3): 1, 2 Corinthians, Ephesians, Philippians, Colossians, Galatians, 1, 2 Thessalonians, and Romans. Then come four Pauline letters to individuals: Philemon, 1, 2 Timothy, and Titus. Then we find the letters to churches in more than one place, the so-called "Catholic Epistles": Jude, 1, 2 John. Finally, there are two apocalypses: Revelation and the Apocalypse of Peter (which, the compiler points out, some do not want read in church).

The list also rejects certain books: Wisdom of Solomon (now in the Apocrypha of the Old Testament!), and the Shepherd of Hermas. The Shepherd is rejected because it is not associated with an apostle, but it was written in Rome about A.D. 135. This popular book may be read privately, but not in church. The list also rejects books, such as a collection of psalms said to come from Marcion. Not mentioned at all are 1, 2 Peter, James, 3 John, and Hebrews.

Rome, of course, was not the only place where churches found it necessary to determine what constituted the New Testament. Similar processes were going on in Egypt and in Asia Minor, and with generally the same results. Only in a few cases, such as James, Second Peter, Hebrews, and Revelation, was there continued discussion of books which were included eventually. There was, of course, also continued debate over a number of books which finally were rejected. But that is another story.

We honor the Jerusalem church because it was formed from the circle of Jesus' original followers and their earliest converts to Christianity. But the church that has actually affected us most—Protestants no less than Catholics—was the church at Rome.